# Breath
# Sweeps
# Mind

TRICYCLE BOOKS FROM RIVERHEAD

**Breath Sweeps Mind**
*A First Guide to Meditation Practice*
*edited by Jean Smith*

**Everyday Mind**
*366 Reflections on the Buddhist Path*
*edited by Jean Smith*

**Wake Up and Cook**
*Kitchen Buddhism in Words and Recipes*
*edited by Carol Tonkinson*

**Meeting the Buddha**
*On Pilgrimage in Buddhist India*
*edited by Molly Emma Aitken*

**Big Sky Mind**
*Buddhism and the Beat Generation*
*edited by Carol Tonkinson*

**Buddhism Without Beliefs**
*A Contemporary Guide to Awakening*
*by Stephen Batchelor*

*Most Riverhead Books are available at special quantity discounts for bulk purchases for sales promotions, premiums, fund-raising or educational use. Special books, or book excerpts, can also be created to fit specific needs.*

*For details write: Special Markets, The Berkley Publishing Group, 200 Madison Avenue, New York, NY 10016.*

# Breath
# Sweeps
# Mind

*A First Guide to Meditation Practice*

*A Tricycle Book*

*Edited by Jean Smith*

*Riverhead Books | New York*

Riverhead Books
Published by The Berkley Publishing Group
A member of Penguin Putnam Inc.
200 Madison Avenue
New York, New York 10016

A continuation of credits appears on pages 269–280.

First Riverhead trade paperback edition: February 1998

The Putnam Berkley World Wide Web site address is
http://www.berkley.com

Library of Congress Cataloging-in-Publication Data
Breath sweeps mind : a first guide to meditation practice / edited by
Jean Smith.—1st Riverhead trade pbk. ed.
p.   cm.
Rev. ed. of: Meditation practice.
"A tricycle book."
Includes index.
ISBN 1-57322-653-X
1. Meditation—Buddhism.   I. Smith, Jean.   II. Meditation
practice.
BQ5612.B74    1998
294.3'4435—dc21                                    97-28036
                                                        CIP

Printed in the United States of America

10   9   8   7   6   5   4   3

*With gratitude, for sangha everywhere*

# Contents

*Preface*    xiii

## Part I:   What Is Meditation?

SOGYAL RINPOCHE *Bringing the Mind Home*    5

THE BUDDHA *The Greater Discourse on the Foundations of Mindfulness*    11

THICH NHAT HANH *The Four Foundations of Mindfulness*    13

JACK KORNFIELD *The Art of Awakening*    17

STEPHEN BATCHELOR *Going Against the Stream*    26

JOHN SNELLING *Buddhist Traditions of Meditation*    29

ZEN MASTER DOGEN *Enlightenment Itself*    37

DAININ KATAGIRI *Mindfulness As the Middle Way*    40

THYNN THYNN *Concentration and Meditation*    44

JON KABAT-ZINN *Stopping and Being Present*    47

JON KABAT-ZINN Exercise/Stopping    49

CHARLOTTE JOKO BECK *What Practice Is Not*    50

CHARLOTTE JOKO BECK *What Practice Is*    53

GARY SNYDER *Just One Breath*    57

VENERABLE HENEPOLA GUNARATANA *The Great Teacher* 60

## Part II:   Why Meditate?

THE BUDDHA *The Greater Discourse on the Foundations of Mindfulness* 65

THE BUDDHA *The Greater Discourse of Advice to [His Son] Rahula* 66

THICH NHAT HANH *To Achieve Necessary Awareness* 69

JOSEPH GOLDSTEIN *To Open, To Balance, To Explore* 72

JOSEPH GOLDSTEIN Exercise/Concepts and Reality 80

AYYA KHEMA *To Transcend Everyday Consciousness* 82

*THE DHAMMAPADA The Mind* 88

B. ALAN WALLACE *To Investigate Reality* 90

JACK KORNFIELD *To Heal the Body, Heart, and Mind* 94

JON KABAT-ZINN *To Pursue Your Vision* 100

SHUNRYU SUZUKI *For Enlightenment* 103

## Part III:   How to Meditate

THE BUDDHA *The Greater Discourse on the Foundations of Mindfulness* 107

JACK KORNFIELD *Establishing a Daily Meditation Practice* 108

# Contents

ix

ZEN MASTER DOGEN *Zen Meditation Instructions*   111

THE DALAI LAMA *Tibetan Meditation Instructions*   113

JOSEPH GOLDSTEIN *Vipassana Meditation Instructions*   116

KOSHO UCHIYAMA *Open the Hand of Thought*   121

JACK KORNFIELD *Sangha and Retreat*   123

## POSTURE   126

VENERABLE HENEPOLA GUNARATANA *What to Do with Your Body*   126

KATHLEEN MCDONALD *Seven-Point Posture*   133

SHUNRYU SUZUKI *The Oneness of Duality*   138

JON KABAT-ZINN *Dignity*   142

## BREATHING   144

THE BUDDHA *Sutra on the Full Awareness of Breathing*   144

ZEN MASTER MAN-AN *Tuning the Breathing*   151

VENERABLE HENEPOLA GUNARATANA *Taming a Wild Elephant*   153

SHUNRYU SUZUKI *The Swinging Door*   158

AYYA KHEMA *Ways of Using the Breath*   160

MAHASI SAYADAW *Exercise/Breathing*   163

## WALKING   166

THE BUDDHA *The Greater Discourse on the Foundations of Mindfulness*   166

# CONTENTS

HAKUIN YASUTANI ROSHI *Kinhin* 168

JOAN HALIFAX *The Mind of Practice Embodied* 170

SYLVIA BOORSTEIN Exercise/Walking 173

## DRIVING 177

THICH NHAT HANH *Driving Meditation* 177

## EATING 180

THICH NHAT HANH: *Eating a Tangerine* 180

JOSEPH GOLDSTEIN Exercise/Eating 183

## USING MANTRAS 186

LEX HIXON *The Heart Sutra* 187

PATRUL RINPOCHE *Mani* 188

NICHIRIN DAISHONIN *The Lotus Sutra* 190

YOSHINORI HIUGA SENSEI *Existence and Unity* 192

SOEN NAKAGAWA *Everything Condensed* 194

## LISTENING 196

SYLVIA BOORSTEIN Exercise/Sound Meditation 196

## VISUALIZATION 198

KATHLEEN MCDONALD *"Thinking" in Pictures* 198

KATHLEEN MCDONALD Exercise/Body of Light
Meditation 203

## FEELINGS AND METTA 205

THYNN THYNN *Attention to Emotions* 205

JOSEPH GOLDSTEIN *Training of the Heart* 208

SHARON SALZBERG *Metta Practice* 211

SHARON SALZBERG Exercise/Lovingkindness 214

## PROBLEMS IN MEDITATING 216

SOGYAL RINPOCHE *The Mind's Own Radiance* 216

THE BUDDHA *Maha-Assapura Sutta* 219

JOSEPH GOLDSTEIN *The Hindrances* 222

HAKUIN YASUTANI ROSHI *Counting Breaths* 231

VENERABLE HENEPOLA GUNARATANA *When the Mind Wanders* 233

JACK KORNFIELD Exercise/Hindrances 239

## POSTSCRIPT

JON KABAT-ZINN *Keeping It Simple* 241

*Buddhist Meditation and Study Centers* 243

*Contributors* 261

*Credits* 269

*Index* 281

# Preface

THERE'S A STORY about a hermit monk many centuries ago who went off to an isolated cave in the
Himalayas to meditate. The first time he sat down to practice there, he found himself staring at a blank gray limestone
wall. So he decided to paint a picture on it before meditating. With infinite care, he created an image of a fierce
tiger on the wall. The tiger looked so realistic that from
then on, every time the monk looked at the wall, he became
frightened. The creations of our mind can be like that.

Two thousand years earlier, another spiritual seeker sat
in isolation to meditate. Like the hapless painter, he too was
assailed by the creations of his mind, but this man—the
Buddha, the Awakened One—saw his "tigers" for what
they were. He saw the truth, and he knew that he *could* see
it because of his experience in meditation. For the next forty

years, the Buddha traveled and taught the truth, and he taught the practice of meditation that is the path to enlightenment.

The Buddha's first instructions are the foundation upon which various Buddhist traditions have built their teachings. *Breath Sweeps Mind: A First Guide to Meditation Practice* brings together these timeless teachings to explore the questions of what meditation is, why one would meditate, and how to establish a meditation practice. Meditation has been called the Great Teacher; and what we can learn from it, as the Buddha did, is the truth.

*Editor's note:* Spellings throughout this collection have been retained from the original sources. Thus, you will find some terms expressed in both Pali, the language spoken in the Buddha's time, and Sanskrit, the language in which many of the teachings were recorded—for example, the Pali *Sutta, Dhamma,* and *Nibbana* and the Sanskrit *Sutra, Dharma,* and *Nirvana.* When teachings from classic sources are given within quotation marks and are not otherwise attributed, the speaker is the Buddha.

# Breath
# Sweeps
# Mind

# Part 1

# What Is Meditation?

# Sogyal Rinpoche

## Bringing the Mind Home

*For thousands of years, spiritual seekers have explored the question
"What is meditation?" One of them, Siddhartha Gautama, the
historical Buddha, discovered that meditation is nothing less than the
path to enlightenment. Tibetan meditation master Sogyal Rinpoche
finds in the Buddha's experience the answers we need in order to
bring our minds into their true nature, to bring our minds home.*

OVER 2,500 YEARS ago, a man who had been
searching for the truth for many, many lifetimes
came to a quiet place in northern India and sat down under a tree. He continued to sit under the tree, with im-
mense resolve, and vowed not to get up until he had
found the truth. At dusk, it is said, he conquered all the
dark forces of delusion, and early the next morning, as
the star Venus broke in the dawn sky, the man was re-
warded for his age-long patience, discipline, and flawless
concentration by achieving the final goal of human existence, enlightenment. At that sacred moment, the earth
itself shuddered, as if "drunk with bliss," and as the
scriptures tell us, "No one anywhere was angry, ill, or
sad; no one did evil, none was proud; the world became
quite quiet, as though it had reached full perfection."

This man became known as the Buddha. Here is the Vietnamese master Thich Nhat Hanh's beautiful description of the Buddha's enlightenment:

> Gautama felt as though a prison which had confined him for thousands of lifetimes had broken open. Ignorance had been the jailkeeper. Because of ignorance, his mind had been obscured, just like the moon and stars hidden by the storm clouds. Clouded by endless waves of deluded thoughts, the mind had falsely divided reality into subject and object, self and others, existence and non-existence, birth and death, and from these discriminations arose wrong views—the prisons of feelings, craving, grasping, and becoming. The suffering of birth, old age, sickness, and death only made the prison walls thicker. The only thing to do was to seize the jailkeeper and see his true face. The jailkeeper was ignorance. . . . Once the jailkeeper was gone, the jail would disappear and never be rebuilt again. [*Old Path, White Clouds*, p. 121]

What the Buddha saw was that ignorance of our true nature is the root of all the torment of samsara ["the uncontrolled cycle of birth and death, that ocean of suffering"], and the root of ignorance itself is our mind's habitual tendency to distraction. To end the mind's distraction would be to end samsara itself; the key to this, he realized, is to bring the mind home to its true nature, through the practice of meditation.

The Buddha sat in serene and humble dignity on the ground, with the sky above him and around him, as if to show us that in meditation you sit with an open, sky-like attitude of mind, yet remain present, earthed, and grounded. The sky is our absolute nature, which has no barriers and is boundless, and the ground is our reality, our relative, ordinary condition. The posture we take when we meditate signifies that we are linking absolute and relative, sky and ground, heaven and earth, like two wings of a bird, integrating the sky-like deathless nature of mind and the ground of our transient, mortal nature.

The gift of learning to meditate is the greatest gift you can give yourself in this life. For it is only through meditation that you can undertake the journey to discover your true nature, and so find the stability and confidence you will need to live, and die, well. Meditation is the road to enlightenment. . . .

Fortunately we live in a time when all over the world many people are becoming familiar with meditation. It is being increasingly accepted as a practice that cuts through and soars above cultural and religious barriers, and enables those who pursue it to establish a direct contact with the truth of their being. It is a practice that at once transcends the dogma of religions and is the essence of religions.

Generally we waste our lives, distracted from our true selves, in endless activity; meditation, on the other hand, is the way to bring us back to ourselves, where we can really experience and taste our full being, beyond all habitual patterns. Our lives are lived in intense and anxious struggle, in a swirl of speed and aggression, in competing, grasping, possessing, and achieving, forever burdening ourselves with extraneous activities and preoccupations. Meditation is the exact opposite. To meditate is to make a complete break with how we "normally" operate, for it is a state free of all cares and concerns, in which there is no competition, no desire to possess or grasp at anything, no intense and anxious struggle, and no hunger to achieve: an ambitionless state where there is neither acceptance nor rejection, neither hope nor fear, a state in which we slowly begin to release all those emotions and concepts that have imprisoned us into the space of natural simplicity.

The Buddhist meditation masters know how flexible and workable the mind is. If we train it, anything is possible. In fact, we are already perfectly trained by and for samsara, trained to get jealous, trained to grasp, trained to be anxious and sad and desperate and greedy, trained to react angrily to whatever provokes us. We are trained, in fact, to such an extent that these negative emotions rise spontaneously, without our even trying to generate them. So everything is a question of training and the power of habit. Devote the mind to confusion and we know only too well, if we're honest, that it will become a dark master of confusion, adept in its addictions, subtle and perversely supple in its slaveries. Devote it in meditation to the task of freeing itself from illusion, and we will find that with time, patience, discipline, and the right training, our mind will begin to unknot itself and know its essential bliss and clarity. . . .

The purpose of meditation is to awaken in us the sky-like nature of mind, and to introduce us to that which we really are, our unchanging pure awareness, which underlies the whole of life and death.

In the stillness and silence of meditation, we glimpse and return to that deep inner nature that we have so long ago lost sight of amid the busyness and distraction of our minds. . . . We are fragmented into so many different aspects. We don't know who we really are, or what aspects of ourselves we should identify with or believe in. So many contradictory voices, dictates, and feelings fight for control over our inner lives that we find ourselves scattered everywhere, in all directions, leaving nobody at home.

Meditation, then, is bringing the mind home. . . .

The whole of meditation practice can be essentialized into these three crucial points: bring your mind home, and release, and relax. Each phrase contains meanings that resonate on many levels.

To *bring your mind home* means to bring the mind into the state of Calm Abiding through the practice of mindfulness. In its deepest sense, to bring your mind home is to turn your mind inward and to rest into the nature of mind. This itself is the highest meditation.

To *release* means to release mind from its prison of grasping, since you recognize that all pain and fear and distress arise from the craving of the grasping mind. On a deeper level, the realization and confidence that arise from your growing understanding of the nature of mind inspire the profound and natural generosity that enables you to release all grasping from your heart, letting it free itself, to melt away in the inspiration of meditation.

Finally, to *relax* means to be spacious and to relax the mind of its tensions.

# The Buddha

## The Greater Discourse on the Foundations of Mindfulness

*The practice by which we learn to bring our mind home, release,
and relax is based on the* Satipatthana *or* Mahasatipatthana Sutta:
The Greater Discourse on the Foundations of Mindfulness.
*In this discourse, the Buddha laid out the basic practices of
meditation for his disciples.*

"THERE IS, MONKS, this one way to the purification
of beings, for the overcoming of sorrow and distress,
for the disappearance of pain and sadness, for the gaining
of the right path, for the realisation of Nibbana:—that is to
say the four foundations of mindfulness.

"What are the four? Here, monks, a monk abides contemplating body as body, ardent, clearly aware and mindful,
having put aside hankering and fretting for the world; he
abides contemplating feelings as feelings . . . ; he abides
contemplating mind as mind . . . ; he abides contemplating
mind-objects as mind-objects, ardent, clearly aware and
mindful, having put aside hankering and fretting for the
world.

"And how, monks, does a monk abide contemplating the

body as body? Here a monk, having gone into the forest, or to the root of a tree, or to an empty place, sits down cross-legged, holding his body erect, having established mindfulness before him.''

# Thich Nhat Hanh

## *The Four Foundations of Mindfulness*

*Vietnamese Zen Buddhist monk Thich Nhat Hanh recounts the
Buddha's teaching to his disciples on the foundations of mindfulness
and explores the meaning of this sermon for
today's practitioners.*

IN THE SPRING of the following year, the Buddha de-
livered the *Satipatthana Sutta*, the *Sutta on the Four Foundations of Mindfulness*, to a gathering of more than three
hundred bhikkhus [monks] in Kammassadhamma, which was
the capital of Kuru. This was a sutra [discourse] fundamental
for the practice of meditation. The Buddha referred to it as
the path which could help every person attain *peace* of body
and mind, overcome all sorrows and lamentations, destroy
suffering and grief, and attain highest understanding and total emancipation. Later, Venerable Sariputta told the community that this was one of the most important sutras the
Buddha had ever given. He encouraged every bhikkhu and
bhikkhuni to study, memorize, and practice it.

Venerable Ananda repeated every word of the sutra later
that night. *Sati* means "to dwell in mindfulness," that is,

the practitioner remains aware of everything taking place in his body, feelings, mind, and objects of mind—the four establishments of mindfulness, or awareness.

First the practitioner observes his body—his breath; the four bodily postures of walking, standing, lying, and sitting; bodily actions such as going forward and backward, looking, putting on robes, eating, drinking, using the toilet, speaking, and washing robes; the parts of the body such as hair, teeth, sinews, bones, internal organs, marrow, intestines, saliva, and sweat; the elements which compose the body such as water, air, and heat; and the stages of a body's decay from the time it dies to when the bones turn to dust.

While observing the body, the practitioner is aware of all details concerning the body. For example, while breathing in, the practitioner knows he is breathing in; breathing out, he knows he is breathing out; breathing in and making his whole body calm and at peace, the practitioner knows he is breathing in and making his whole body calm and at peace. Walking, the practitioner knows he is walking. Sitting, the practitioner knows he is sitting. Performing movements such as putting on robes or drinking water, the practitioner knows he is putting on robes or drinking water. The contemplation of the body is not realized only during the moments of sitting meditation, but throughout the entire day, including the moments one is begging, eating, and washing one's bowl.

In the contemplation of feelings, the practitioner contemplates feelings as they arise, develop, and fade, feelings which are pleasant, unpleasant, or neutral. Feelings can have as their source either the body or the mind. When he feels pain from a toothache, the practitioner is aware that he feels pain from a toothache; when he is happy because he has received praise, the practitioner is aware that he is happy because he has received praise. The practitioner looks deeply in order to calm and quiet every feeling in order to clearly see the sources which give rise to feelings. The contemplation of feelings does not take place only during the moments of sitting meditation. It is practiced throughout the day.

In the contemplation of mind, the practitioner contemplates the presence of his mental states. Craving, he knows he is craving; not craving, he knows he is not craving. Angry or drowsy, he knows he is angry or drowsy; not angry or drowsy, he knows he is not angry or drowsy. Centered or distracted, he knows he is centered or distracted. Whether he is open-minded, close-minded, blocked, concentrated, or enlightened, the practitioner knows at once. And if he is not experiencing any of those states, the practitioner also knows at once. The practitioner recognizes and is aware of every mental state which arises within him in the present moment.

In the contemplation of the objects of mind, the practitioner contemplates the five hindrances to liberation (sense-desire, ill-will, drowsiness, agitation, and doubt) whenever they are present; the five skandhas [aggregates] which comprise a person (body, feelings, perceptions, mental formations, and consciousness); the six sense organs and the six sense objects; the Seven Factors of Awakening (full attention, investigating dharmas [phenomena], energy, joy, ease, concentration, and letting-go); and the Four Noble Truths (the existence of suffering, the causes of suffering, liberation from suffering, and the path that leads to liberation from suffering). These are all objects of the mind, and they contain all dharmas.

The Buddha carefully explained each of the four establishments. He said that whoever practiced these four establishments for seven years would attain emancipation. He added that anyone who practiced them for seven months could also attain emancipation. He said that even after practicing these four contemplations for seven days, one could attain emancipation.

# Jack Kornfield

## The Art of Awakening

*With the Buddha's basic teachings on meditation practice in mind, we turn to American Vipassana teacher Jack Kornfield for guidance in developing our own personal path to emancipation.*

A STORY IS TOLD of the Buddha when he was wandering in India shortly after his enlightenment. He was encountered by several men who recognized something quite extraordinary about this handsome prince now robed as a monk. Stopping to inquire, they asked, "Are you a god?" "No," he answered. "Well, are you a deva or an angel?" "No," he replied. "Well, are you some kind of wizard or magician?" "No." "Are you a man?" "No." They were perplexed. Finally they asked, "Then what are you?" He replied simply, "I am awake." The word *Buddha* means to awaken. How to awaken is all he taught.

Meditation can be thought of as the art of awakening. Through the mastering of this art we can learn new ways to approach our difficulties and bring wisdom and joy alive in our life. Through developing meditation's tools and practices, we can awaken the best of our spiritual, human capacities. The key to this art is the steadiness of our attention.

When the fullness of our attention is cultivated together with a grateful and tender heart, our spiritual life will naturally grow.

. . . [S]ome healing of mind and body must take place for many of us before we can sit quietly and concentrate. Yet even to begin our healing, to begin understanding ourselves, we must have some basic level of attention. To deepen our practice further, we must choose a way to develop our attention systematically and give ourselves to it quite fully. Otherwise we will drift like a boat without a rudder. To learn to concentrate we must choose a prayer or meditation and follow this path with commitment and steadiness, a willingness to work with our practice day after day, no matter what arises. This is not easy for most people. They would like their spiritual life to show immediate and cosmic results. But what great art is ever learned quickly? Any deep training opens in direct proportion to how much we give ourselves to it.

Consider the other arts. Music, for example. How long would it take to learn to play the piano well? Suppose we take months or years of lessons once a week, practicing diligently every day. Initially, almost everyone struggles to learn which fingers go for which notes and how to read basic lines of music. After some weeks or months, we could play simple tunes, and perhaps after a year or two we could play a chosen type of music. However, to master the art so that we could play music well, alone or in a group, or join a band or an orchestra, we would have to give ourselves to this discipline over and over, time and again. If we wanted to learn computer programming, oil painting, tennis, architecture, any of the thousand arts, we would have to give ourselves to it fully and wholeheartedly over a long period of time—a training, an apprenticeship, a cultivation.

Nothing less is required in the spiritual arts. Perhaps even more is asked. Yet through this mastery we master ourselves and our lives. We learn the most human art, how to connect with our truest self. . . .

Suppose we begin with a period of solitude in the midst of our daily life. What happens when we actually try to meditate? The most frequent first experience—whether in prayer or chanting, meditation or visualization—is that we encounter the disconnected and scattered mind. Buddhist psychology likens the untrained mind to a crazed monkey that dashes from thought to memory, from sight to sound, from plan to regret without ceasing. If we were able to sit quietly for an hour and fully observe all the places our mind went, what a script would be revealed. . . .

In this way, meditation is very much like training a puppy. You put the puppy down and say, "Stay." Does the puppy listen? It gets up and it runs away. You sit the puppy back down again. "Stay." And the puppy runs away over and over again. Sometimes the puppy jumps up, runs over, and pees in the corner or makes some other mess. Our minds are much the same as the puppy, only they create even bigger messes. In training the mind, or the puppy, we have to start over and over again.

When you undertake a spiritual discipline, frustration comes with the territory. Nothing in our culture or our schooling has taught us to steady and calm our attention. . . . Finding it difficult to concentrate, many people respond by forcing their attention on their breath or mantra or prayer with tense irritation and self-judgment, or worse. Is this the way you would train a puppy? Does it really help to beat it? Concentration is never a matter of force or coercion. You simply pick up the puppy again and return to reconnect with the here and now.

Developing a deep quality of interest in your spiritual practice is one of the keys to the whole art of concentration. Steadiness is nourished by the degree of interest with which we focus our meditation. Yet, to the beginning student, many meditation subjects appear plain and uninteresting. There is a traditional story about a Zen student who complained to his master that following the breath was boring. The Zen master grabbed this student and held his head under water for quite a long time while the student struggled to come up. When he finally let the student up, the Zen master asked him whether he had found breath boring in those moments under water. . . .

The focusing of attention on the breath is perhaps the most universal of the many hundreds of meditation subjects used worldwide. . . . Breathing meditation can quiet the mind, open the body, and develop a great power of concentration. The breath is available to us at any time of day and in any circumstance. When we have learned to use it, the breath becomes a support for awareness throughout our life. . . .

Yet even with interest and a strong desire to steady our attention, distractions will arise. Distractions are the natural movement of mind. Distractions arise because our mind and heart are not initially clear or pure. Mind is more like muddy or turbulent water. Each time an enticing image or an interesting memory floats by, it is our habit to react, to get entangled, or to get lost. When painful images or feelings arise, it is our habit to avoid them and unknowingly distract ourselves. We can feel the power of these habits of desire, of distracting ourselves, of fear and reaction. In many of us these forces are so great that after a few unfamiliar moments of calm, our mind rebels. Again and again restlessness, busyness, plans, unfelt feelings, all interrupt our focus. Working with these distractions, steadying the canoe, letting the waves pass by, and coming back again and again in a quiet and collected way, is at the heart of meditation.

After your initial trial, you will begin to recognize that certain external conditions are particularly helpful in developing concentration. Finding or creating a quiet and undistracting place for your practice is necessary. Select regular and suitable times that best fit your temperament and schedule; experiment to discover whether morning or evening meditations best support the silent aspects of your inner life. You may wish to begin with a short period of inspiring reading before sitting, or do some stretching or yoga first. Some people find it extremely helpful to sit in a regular group with others or to go off to periodic retreats. Experiment with these external factors until you discover which are most helpful for your own inner peace. Then make them a regular part of your life. Creating suitable conditions means living wisely, providing the best soil for our spiritual hearts to be nourished and to grow.

As we give ourselves to the art of concentration over the weeks and months, we discover that our concentration slowly begins to settle by itself. . . . As we continue, the development of concentration brings us closer to life, like the focusing of a lens. When we look at pond water in a cup, it appears clear and still. But under the simplest microscope it shows itself to be alive with creatures and movement. In the same way, the more deeply we pay attention, the less solid our breath and body become. Every place we feel breath in our body can come alive with subtle vibrations, movement, tingles, flow. The steady power of our concentration shows each part of our life to be in change and flux, like a river even as we feel it.

As we learn to let go into the present, the breath breathes itself, allowing the flow of sensations in the body to move and open. There can come an openness and ease. Like a skilled dancer, we allow the breath and body to float and move unhindered, yet all the while being present to enjoy the opening.

As we become more skillful we also discover that concentration has its own seasons. Sometimes we sit and settle easily. At other times the conditions of mind and body are turbulent or tense. We can learn to navigate all these waters. When conditions show the mind is tight, we learn to soften and relax, to open the attention. When the mind is sleepy or flabby, we learn to sit up and focus with more energy. The Buddha compared this with the tuning of a lute, sensing when we are out of tune and gently strengthening or loosening our energy to come into balance.

In learning concentration, we feel as if we are always starting over, always losing our focus. But where have we actually gone? It is only that a mood or a thought or doubt has swept through our mind. As soon as we recognize this, we can let go and settle back again in this next moment. We can always begin again. Gradually as our interest grows and our capacity to sense deepens, new layers of our meditation open. We will find ourselves alternating, discovering periods of deep peace like an undisturbed child and strength like a great ship on a true course, only to be distracted or lost sometime later. . . .

Always remember that in training a puppy we want to end up with the puppy as our friend. In the same way, we must practice seeing our mind and body as "friend." Even its wanderings can be included in our meditation with a friendly interest and curiosity. Right away we can notice how it moves. The mind produces waves. Our breath is a wave, the sensations of our body are a wave. We don't have to fight the waves. We can simply acknowledge, "Surf's up." "Here's the wave of memories from three years old." "Here's the planning wave." Then it's time to reconnect with the wave of the breath. It takes a gentleness and a kindhearted understanding to deepen the art of concentration. We can't be present for a long period without actually softening, dropping into our bodies, coming to rest. Any other kind of concentration, achieved by force and tension, will only be short-lived. Our task is to train the puppy to become our lifelong friend.

The attitude or spirit with which we do our meditation helps us perhaps more than any other aspect. What is called for is a sense of perseverance and dedication combined with a basic friendliness. We need a willingness to directly relate again and again to what is actually here, with a lightness of heart and sense of humor. We do not want the training of our puppy to become too serious a matter.

The Christian Desert Fathers tell of a new student who was commanded by his master that for three years he must give money to everyone who insulted him. When this period of trial was over, the master said, "Now you can go to Alexandria and truly learn wisdom." When the student entered Alexandria, he met a certain wise man whose way of teaching was to sit at the city gate insulting everyone who came and went. He naturally insulted the student also, who immediately burst out laughing. "Why do you laugh when I insult you?" said the wise man. "Because," said the student, "for years I've been paying for this kind of thing, and now you give it to me for free!'' ''Enter the city,'' said the wise man. ''It is all yours.''

Meditation is a practice that can teach us to enter each moment with wisdom, lightness, and a sense of humor. It is an art of opening and letting go, rather than accumulation or struggle. Then, even within our frustrations and difficulties, a remarkable inner sense of support and perspective can grow. Breathing in, ''Wow, this experience is interesting, isn't it? Let me take another breath. Ah, this one is difficult, even terrifying, isn't it?'' Breathing out, ''Ah.'' It is an amazing process we have entered when we can train our hearts and minds to be open and steady and awake through it all.

# Stephen Batchelor

## Going Against the Stream

*Training our hearts and minds in meditation practice is like swimming upstream against a powerful current, notes British scholar and teacher Stephen Batchelor. The basic techniques taught by the Buddha for this effort toward freedom underlie all the traditions that have evolved from his earliest teachings.*

THE TRAINING IN mindful awareness is part of a Buddhist path with values and goals. Emotional states are evaluated according to whether they increase or decrease the potential for suffering. If an emotion, such as hatred or envy, is judged to be destructive, then it is simply recognized as such. It is neither expressed through violent thoughts, words or deeds, nor is it suppressed or denied as incompatible with a "spiritual" life. In seeing it for what it is—a transient emotional state—one mindfully observes it follow its own nature: to arise, abide for a while, and then pass away.

The Buddha described his teaching as "going against the stream." The unflinching light of mindful awareness reveals the extent to which we are tossed along in the stream of past conditioning and habit. The moment we decide to stop and look at what is going on (like a swimmer suddenly changing course to swim upstream instead of downstream), we find ourselves battered by powerful currents we had never even suspected—precisely because until that moment we were largely living at their command.

The practice of mindful awareness is a first step in the direction of inner freedom. Disciplining oneself to focus attention single-mindedly on the breath (for example) enables one to become progressively more quiet and concentrated. Such stillness, though, is not an end in itself. It serves as a platform from which to observe more clearly what is taking place within us. It allows the steady depth of awareness needed to understand the very origins of conditioning: namely, how delusion and craving are at the root of human suffering. Such meditative understanding is experiential rather than intellectual, therapeutic rather than dogmatic, liberating rather than merely convincing.

The aim of mindful awareness is the understanding that frees one from delusion and craving. In Pali, such understanding is called *vipassana* ("penetrative seeing"), and it is under this name that the traditional practice of mindful awareness is frequently presented in the West today. *Vipassana* is often translated as "insight," and courses are offered on "insight meditation."

This usage has given rise to some confusion. It has led to the impression that some Buddhists practice *vipassana,* while others (such as practitioners of Zen or Tibetan Buddhism) do not. In fact, *vipassana* is central to *all* forms of Buddhist meditation practice. The distinctive goal of any Buddhist contemplative tradition is a state in which inner calm *(sa-matha)* is *unified* with insight *(vipassana)*. Over the centuries, each tradition has developed its own methods for actualizing this state. And it is in these methods that the traditions differ, *not* in their end objective of unified calm and insight.

# John Snelling

## Buddhist Traditions of Meditation

*In the 2,500 years since the Buddha taught his disciples the
foundations of mindfulness, the basic goals have not changed, but
British writer John Snelling traces how the methods of practice have
evolved in the major traditions, from Theravada Vipassana to
Japanese Pure Land and Zen to Tibetan Tantra.*

WHAT IS MEDITATION?
Remember Dr. Johnson's pithy dictum: "Depend
upon it, sir, when a man knows he is to be hanged, it
concentrates his mind wonderfully." The truth is, we live
our lives in a kind of waking dream. We are only hazily
aware of what is really going on both outside and, even
more so, inside ourselves. Every chance stimulus—every
random meeting or event, every vagrant emotion, mood,
impulse, and so on—just sparks off a more or less automatic
reaction. It needs a vital shock, like a stark confrontation
with death, to jerk us awake. Then for a moment the scales
of semi-sleep, subjectivity, projection and fantasy fall from
our eyes and we see the world as it *really* is.

Meditation is about developing that kind of acute awareness all the time. And it means doing so without becoming

attached to the objects of observation out of desire, or rejecting them from aversion. It means becoming the dispas-
sionate watcher, the one who knows: becoming Buddha, in
fact. . . .


## MINDFULNESS

The basic form of meditation that the early texts describe
the Buddha as teaching is not sitting meditation, as one
might have expected from modern formal practice, but
something to be done by a monk as he "fares along," going
about his normal business. It consists of the specific appli-
cations of Mindfulness, described by the Buddha in the *Satipatthana Sutta*. . . .


## SHAMATHA AND VIPASHYANA

Later systematizers and the compilers of Buddhist medita-
tion manuals subdivided meditation practice into two parts:
Shamatha (Calm Abiding) and Vipashyana (Insight or Higher
Vision). In the Pali language they are known as Samatha and
Vipassana.

Shamatha is concerned with developing concentration—
that is, the ability to maintain the focus of attention one-
pointedly but without undue exertion on a chosen object—

and with calming and stabilizing the mind so that it is no longer disturbed by deluding excitations. . . .

In Vipashyana or Insight Meditation, the calmness and concentrative ability forged in Shamatha are used to inquire penetratively into the true nature of things. Intense observation and analysis of phenomena encountered will, according to the classic texts, reveal that all are subject to duhkha [suffering], anitya [impermanence] and anatman [nonself]; are inherently painful or unsatisfactory, impermanent and devoid of atman or self—or put simply: "everything that arises passes away and is not self." This is not mere head-knowledge but a deep existential understanding that is at once purifying and liberating. More positively, it is said to also give access to the Unconditioned: to Nirvana. . . .

## MAHAYANA BUDDHIST MEDITATION

Mahayana Buddhism . . . has rather different objectives from those of the early schools. . . . [T]he devotees of the Mahayana aspire to a similarly profound penetration of the truth of Shunyata, Emptiness, and make this a primary object of meditation. They also seek to generate bodhisattvic [enlightened being] qualities so that they can work effectively in Samsara to alleviate the suffering of sentient beings. Yet for all that the meditation methods of most Mahayana schools rest firmly on a basis of Mindfulness and Shamatha-Vipashyana. . . .

## PURE LAND MEDITATION

On the face of it, the devotional Pure Land school might seem to have little to do with meditation. Its devotees take the view that, in the dark age in which we are living, we can hope to attain little by our own striving. All we can do is to throw ourselves on the mercy of the celestial buddha Amitabha. Where our "self power" (Japanese, *jiriki*) is impotent, his "other power" (Japanese, *tariki*) can save us by ensuring our rebirth in the Pure Land of Sukhavati.

Most of the Pure Land that has been transmitted to the West is of the Japanese variety, represented by the Jodo and the Jodo-shin schools, which place primary emphasis on the Nembutsu: the repetition of the name of Amitabha (Japanese, Amida). Such a practice must pacify thoughts and establish mental calmness, mindfulness and concentration.

Previously, in China, where Pure Land Buddhism came fully into its own, some of the early masters used more sophisticated methods of meditation, such as visualizing Amitabha and his Pure Land and even formless kinds of meditation, which were thought to produce meditative states no less profound than those produced by the practices of other schools, such as the Zen school.

## ZEN MEDITATION

The Zen school, known in China as Ch'an, might be called the meditation school par excellence. Ostensibly disparaging scriptural learning (though in fact squarely rooted in Yogacara and Prajnaparamita philosophy) and other practices (like performing rituals, reciting the scriptures, and so on), it emphasizes direct seeing into one's own nature. The early Chinese Zen masters do not especially recommend sitting meditation; direct seeing can be accomplished—and sustained—in everyday life. However, later Chinese and Japanese Zen stressed the importance of zazen or sitting meditation—and lots of it, both by day and at night. This, according to the Japanese master Dogen, is the "front gate of the Buddha-dharma [Buddha-law]" and "not just the practice of one or two buddhas; all buddhas and ancestors follow this way." Hakuin, another Japanese master, meanwhile says that all other practices come back to sitting meditation, and that "by the merits of a single sitting" the practitioner "destroys innumerable accumulated sins."

Legend has it that Zen originated in India, but really it came into its own in T'ang dynasty China. Of the so-called "Five Houses" that flourished then, only two have survived to the present, but these have been successfully transmitted to the West via Japan. These are the Lin-chi (Japanese, Rinzai) and the Ts'ao-tung (Japanese, Soto).

Soto Zen meditation (Shikan-taza) is usually practiced facing a blank wall. The internal method—sticklers would no doubt call it a non-method—is essentially formless. Dogen, who transmitted the teachings of the school from China to Japan, declares that zazen is not learning to do concentration. It is not introspection. It is not thinking of good or bad. It is not a conscious endeavor of any kind. There should not be expectations. One should not even desire to become a buddha. Just—

Sit solidly in meditation and think not-thinking. How do you think not-thinking? Nonthinking. This is the art of zazen.

. . . Meditation in the Rinzai tradition, on the other hand, is rather more militant. Practitioners sit in straight lines, facing each other. They begin perhaps with a Shamatha-type breath-watching or counting practice to bring about calmness and concentration. Then they traditionally apply themselves with concerted effort to koan practice.

Koan riddles (Chinese, kung-an) are generally based on the records of real life situations in which early masters enlightened their students. In Sung dynasty China, as Zen began to lose its original flair and vitality, these were collected in great anthologies like the *Blue Cliff Record* and the *Gateless Gate*. These formalized riddles, now having something of the significance of precedents in case law, are still handed out to Rinzai Zen practitioners today. Pondering them long and deeply, the student will attempt to give an "answer" to the teacher, usually in Japan called a roshi or "old master," in the course of regular interviews (sanzen). The roshi will then judge its authenticity. Any "answer" that smacks however slightly of conceptualization or phony contrivance will be ruthlessly rejected. If, however, the devotee comes up with an acceptable answer, he or she may well be adjudged to have had a genuine breakthrough or satori. But that is just the beginning. More work must be done to deepen understanding. In other words, once a degree of calmness, clarity and concentration has been produced, the koan is an extremely active device for continually throwing the student against the ultimate question of his own nature.

## TANTRIC MEDITATION

[Tibetan] Buddhist Tantra aims at bringing about Enlightenment very speedily by special yogic means. It is not, however, according to its own teachings, suited to everyone. Only special candidates who have already practiced long and successfully gained deep insight into Shunyata (Emptiness) as well as having developed a high degree of bodhicitta qualify to practice it. Then they must forge a connection with a learned guru, who will initiate them into the mandala [symbolic cosmology] or sacred precinct of their chosen deity (yidam). The rite of initiation (abhisheka) that the guru bestows allows the devotee to perform a range of specialized rituals and practices (sadhana), many of which involve working with dark aspects of the psyche. Herein lie special dangers, so both to protect the unwary from burning themselves and the teachings from being debased Tantra is hedged around with a veil of secrecy, grave vows and other protections. . . .

Insofar as Tantra involves meditation it presupposes a solid basis in Mindfulness and Shamatha-Vipashyana (known in Tibetan as Shine-Lhatong). Given these, its own distinctive practices involve creative visualization, which is carried out to a virtuoso degree of proficiency. The devotee will learn, for instance, to create the form of his chosen deity out of the bija or seed mantra that embodies the essence of the deity, the bija being firstly created out of the Emptiness of his own mind. The mental image of the deity must be built up in very precise detail and full color according to archetypal patterns.

# Zen Master Dogen

## Enlightenment Itself

*The thirteenth-century Zen master Dogen, the most important
teacher in the history of Buddhism in Japan, disregarded the view
that certain elements ran through meditation up to the moment of
realization. Rather, he saw meditation as enlightenment itself.*

TRUTH IS PERFECT and complete in itself. It is not
something newly discovered; it has always existed.

Truth is not far away; it is ever present. It is not something to be attained since not one of your steps leads away
from it.

Do not follow the ideas of others, but learn to listen to
the voice within yourself. Your body and mind will become
clear and you will realize the unity of all things.

The slightest movement of your dualistic thought will
prevent you from entering the palace of meditation and
wisdom.

The Buddha meditated for six years, Bodhidharma for
nine. The practice of meditation is not a method for the
attainment of realization—it is enlightenment itself.

Your search among books, word upon word, may lead

you to the depths of knowledge but it is not the way to receive the reflection of your true self.

When you have thrown off your ideas as to mind and body, the original truth will fully appear. Zen is simply the expression of truth; therefore, longing and striving are not the true attitudes of Zen.

To actualize the blessedness of meditation, you should practice with pure intention and firm determination. Your meditation room should be clean and quiet. Do not dwell in thoughts of good or bad. Just relax and forget that you are meditating. Do not desire realization since that thought will keep you confused.

Sit on a cushion in a manner as comfortable as possible, wearing loose clothing. Hold your body straight without leaning to the left or the right, forward or backward. Your ears should be in line with your shoulders, and your nose in a straight line with your navel. Keep your tongue at the roof of your mouth and close your lips. Keep your eyes slightly open, and breathe through your nostrils.

Before you begin meditation take several slow, deep breaths. Hold your body erect, allowing your breathing to become normal again. Many thoughts will crowd into your mind; ignore them, letting them go. If they persist be aware of them with the awareness that does not think. In other words, think non-thinking.

Zen meditation is not physical culture, nor is it a method to gain something material. It is peacefulness and blessedness itself. It is the actualization of truth and wisdom.

In your meditation you yourself are the mirror reflecting the solution of your problems. The human mind has absolute freedom within its true nature. You can attain your freedom intuitively. Do not work for freedom, rather allow the practice itself to be liberation.

When you wish to rest, move your body slowly and stand up quietly. Practice this meditation in the morning or in the evening, or at any leisure time during the day. You will soon realize that your mental burdens are dropping away one by one, and that you are gaining an intuitive power hitherto unnoticed.

There are thousands upon thousands of students who have practiced meditation and obtained its fruits. Do not doubt its possibilities because of the simplicity of the method. If you cannot find the truth right where you are, where else do you expect to find it?

Life is short and no one knows what the next moment will bring. Open your mind while you have the opportunity, thereby gaining the treasures of wisdom, which in turn you can share abundantly with others, bringing them happiness.

# Dainin Katagiri

## Mindfulness As the Middle Way

*Seven centuries after Dogen, another Japanese Zen master, Dainin Katagiri, found the freedom of enlightenment in daily life by practicing the Middle Way.*

THE MIDDLE WAY is the central teaching of the Buddha. It is not merely walking in the middle of the street. The Middle Way is the state of human body and mind working freely.

One way to understand the Middle Way is that it is the middle point, which is equal in distance from both ends of a line. This means when you get to the middle point you can see both sides, one on the left and one on the right, equally distant. In other words, you can see equally both good and bad, right and wrong. Whatever happens, if you are in the middle you can see both sides in the dualistic world equally. If you stay on the side called "good," or on the side called "evil," you cannot see either of them. In Japan, this is called *tan pan kan,* a board-carrying fellow. A man who carries a board on his shoulder can see only one side. The other side is the aspect of life he cannot see. Human life exists in the dualistic world of good and bad, right and wrong. We cannot stay on either side. But even though we cannot do this, it doesn't mean we should ignore good or bad, right or wrong. We have to understand both sides. In order to approach the destination, the beautiful, ideal image of human life that we call bodhisattva life or freedom, our mind must not be paralyzed. We don't know what freedom is, but more or less we are really seeking freedom. In order to reach freedom we have to see both sides of the dualistic world and handle both sides in equality. This is wisdom or the Middle Way.

Another way to understand the Middle Way is that it is the center of a ball. A ball is constantly changing, rolling, acting. This is human life. Human beings never stop acting. Whatever you are doing—sitting, sleeping, even standing still—you are always acting. Without action, you do not exist. It is just like a ball that is constantly going here and there or standing still according to circumstances. When a slope comes, the ball rolls down the hill. It acts, but even though it appears to be moving, the center is always still. We call this stillness *samadhi*. It is like the center of a torpedo. A torpedo is centered in front, and this center suggests which direction the torpedo should go. This means its center is always still, like the center of a ball. On the other hand, the center is not still. The center must be dynamic; it works, it acts. We call this dynamic centeredness, mindfulness.

In Theravada and Mahayana Buddhism, the practice of mindfulness is very important. Mindfulness is very closely related to samadhi and wisdom. If we are without mindfulness we cannot have samadhi, which is perfect stillness.

Zazen is the basic practice that allows us to experience exactly what perfect stillness is. It is very difficult to experience this stillness without zazen. But you can experience samadhi in your daily life through mindfulness. Mindfulness has exactly the same meaning as "not to forget." "Not to forget" means to think, be mindful of something, be mindful of not forgetting. In our daily life it is pretty easy for us to be mindful of some things, for instance, playing ball, gambling at the races or at poker. It is pretty easy to be mindful and forget the time. We can be mindful of some things, but it is not always good. It is very difficult for us to be mindful of something good.

The Buddha says to be mindful of Dharma. Dharma is that which makes it possible for everything to exist. In other words, Dharma is the basic nature of existence. So, to be mindful of Dharma is to be mindful of that which maintains existence. To maintain something is a function of the dualistic world, because to act, to maintain is, generally speaking, to have an object. So, to be mindful of Dharma means when you do gassho [a greeting of respect, with the palms brought together], be mindful of gassho. When you walk on the street, be mindful of walking.

Mindfulness is to go toward the center, whatever you are doing. Usually the mind is going in many directions; instead of going out in all directions, let's go in. This means, look at the walking itself that you are doing now. This is to move toward the beautiful, ideal image of human life. It is Buddhist practice in zazen and in everyday life.

# Thynn Thynn

## Concentration and Meditation

*When Burmese Theravadan teacher Thynn Thynn considers Buddhist practice in everyday life, she draws a sharp distinction between concentration, or the collected mind, and meditation, in which the collected mind moves toward insight-wisdom.*

FOR MANY PEOPLE the act of concentration is synonymous with meditation. That is probably the reason why so many good Buddhists are more or less satisfied with the notion that when they are doing something in a concentrated fashion—such as reading, working, playing golf—they are already meditating. They are partly right and partly wrong.

Actually, concentration is only a part of meditation. The essence of meditation is to reach a higher form of understanding, *panna,* to stretch the mind beyond the boundaries of the intellect into the realm of the intuitive, of insight-wisdom. In most cases, meditative disciplines require collecting the mind to a one-pointed state in the initial stages. The first method used is to train the mind to concentrate on one single object.

If one considers the pure act of concentration one uses in one's work or hobby, one sees that the objective of such a feat is quite different from that of meditation. In our work or hobby we are merely concerned with accomplishing something that is outside of us generally, like job success, winning a game of golf, completing a scientific experiment, etc. In meditation, however, the achievement is inward, an achievement of self-understanding and spiritual insight. In the initial stages of meditation it may be necessary to concentrate on objects that are external to one's mind, like on the nostrils, or on the movement of the abdomen, until the mind is collected at one point. This type of one-pointed collectedness also occurs while we work or play, but that's where the similarity between concentration and meditation ends.

Concentration is pure and simple collectedness of the mind, whereas meditation is the collected mind moving further toward the development of insight-wisdom, or *vipassana*. In meditation, the awareness of the mind automatically shifts onto the mind itself and of its own accord focuses on its workings and processes, ultimately leading to true self-knowledge.

Though we may come to some form of understanding while concentrating on work and play, this type of knowledge or understanding is intellect-bound, whereas meditative knowledge is intuitive and spiritual. Therefore, the two kinds of understanding are entirely different in nature and serve completely different purposes.

In pure concentration, there is always duality in the mind—"I" and "what I am doing." There is a subject, an object and the process of doing. In other words, there is the knower, the known and the knowing. Meditation also begins with these three. But eventually the mind transcends these divisions by turning inward toward itself. The ultimate enlightenment experience is the state where the differentiation of knower, the known and the knowing ceases.

To confuse concentration with meditation leads to the difficult-to-overcome states of apathy and self-satisfaction. Thus, the concept that concentration and meditation are the same is a misunderstanding that offers us no help on the path to liberation, and may even hamper aspirants in their inner progress.

# Jon Kabat-Zinn

## Stopping and Being Present

*To achieve that moment when the knower, the known, and the knowing become one, American Jon Kabat-Zinn stresses the simplicity—and the challenge—of stopping and being present for our lives.*

PEOPLE THINK OF meditation as some kind of special activity, but this is not exactly correct. Meditation is simplicity itself. As a joke, we sometimes say: "Don't just do something, sit there." But meditation is not just about sitting, either. It is about stopping and being present, that is all. Mostly we run around doing. Are you able to come to a stop in your life, even for one moment? Could it be this moment? What would happen if you did?

A good way to stop all the doing is to shift into the "being mode" for a moment. Think of yourself as an eternal witness, as timeless. Just watch this moment, without trying to change it at all. What is happening? What do you feel? What do you see? What do you hear?

The funny thing about stopping is that as soon as you do it, here you are. Things get simpler. In some ways, it's as if you died and the world continued on. If you did die, all your responsibilities and obligations would immediately evaporate. Their residue would somehow get worked out without you. No one else can take over your unique agenda. It would die or peter out with you just as it has for everyone else who has ever died. So you don't need to worry about it in any absolute way.

If this is true, maybe you don't need to make one more phone call right now, even if you think you do. Maybe you don't need to read something just now, or run one more errand. By taking a few moments to "die on purpose" to the rush of time while you are still living, you free yourself to have time for the present. By "dying" now in this way, you actually become more alive now. This is what stopping can do. There is nothing passive about it. And when you decide to go, it's a different kind of going because you stopped. The stopping actually makes the going more vivid, richer, more textured. It helps keep all the things we worry about and feel inadequate about in perspective. It gives us guidance.

# Jon Kabat-Zinn

## *Exercise / Stopping*

TRY: STOPPING, SITTING down, and becoming aware of your breathing once in a while throughout the day. It can be for five minutes, or even five seconds. Let go into full acceptance of the present moment, including how you are feeling and what you perceive to be happening. For these moments, don't try to change anything at all, just breathe and let go. Breathe and let be. Die to having to have anything be different in this moment; in your mind and in your heart, give yourself permission to allow this moment to be exactly as it is, and allow yourself to be exactly as you are. Then, when you're ready, move in the direction your heart tells you to go, mindfully and with resolution.

# Charlotte Joko Beck

## What Practice Is Not

*When we do stop and rest in the moment, we are practicing.*
*However, as American Zen teacher Charlotte Joko Beck notes, if*
*stopping is part of an agenda to achieve another end, it is not*
*practice.*

MANY PEOPLE PRACTICE and have strong ideas of what practice is. What I want to do is to state (from my point of view) what practice is *not*.

First, practice is not about producing psychological change. If we practice with intelligence, psychological change *will* be produced; I'm not questioning that—in fact, it's wonderful. I am saying that practice is not done in order to produce such change.

Practice is not about intellectually knowing the physical nature of reality, what the universe consists of, or how it works. And again, in serious practice, we will tend to have some knowledge of such matters. But that is not what practice is.

Practice is not about achieving some blissful state. It's not about having visions. It's not about seeing white lights (or pink or blue ones). All of these things may occur, and if we sit long enough they probably will. But that is not what practice is about.

Practice is not about having or cultivating special powers. There are many of these and we all have some of them naturally; some people have them in extra measure. At the Zen Center of Los Angeles (ZCLA) I sometimes had the useful ability to see what was being served for dinner two doors away. If they were having something I didn't like, I didn't go. Such abilities are little oddities, and again they are not what practice is about.

Practice is not about personal power or *joriki,* the strength that is developed in years of sitting. Again, *joriki* is a natural by-product of zazen. And again it is not the way.

Practice is not about having nice feelings, happy feelings. It's not about feeling good as opposed to feeling bad. It's not an attempt to be anything special or to feel anything special. The product of practice or the point of practice or what practice is about is not to be always calm and collected. Again, we tend to be much more so after years of practice, but it is not the point.

Practice is not about some bodily state in which we are never ill, never hurt, one in which we have no bothersome ailments. Sitting tends to have health benefits for many people, though in the course of practice there may be months or even years of health disasters. But again, seeking perfect health is not the way; although by and large, over time, there will be a beneficial effect on health for most people. But no guarantees!

Practice is not about achieving an omniscient state in which a person knows all about everything, a state in which a person is an authority on any and all worldly problems. There may be a little more clarity on such matters, but clever people have been known to say and do foolish things. Again, omniscience is not the point.

Practice is not about being "spiritual," at least not as this word is often understood. Practice is not about being *anything*. So unless we see that we cannot aim at being "spiritual," it can be a seductive and harmful objective.

Practice is not about highlighting all sorts of "good" qualities and getting rid of the so-called "bad" ones. No one is "good" or "bad." The struggle to be good is not what practice is. That type of training is a subtle form of athleticism.

We could continue our listing almost endlessly. Actually anyone in practice has some of these delusions operating. We all hope to change, to get somewhere! That in itself is the basic fallacy. But just contemplating this desire begins to clarify it, and the practice basis of our life alters as we do so. We begin to comprehend that our frantic desire to get better, to "get somewhere," is illusion itself, and the source of suffering.

If our boat full of hope, illusions, and ambition (to get somewhere, to be spiritual, to be perfect, to be enlightened) is capsized, what is that empty boat? Who are we? What, in terms of our lives, can we realize? And what is practice?

# Charlotte Joko Beck

## *What Practice Is*

PRACTICE IS VERY simple. That doesn't mean it won't turn our life around, however. . . . Sitting is essentially a simplified space. Our daily life is in constant movement: lots of things going on, lots of people talking, lots of events taking place. In the middle of that, it's very difficult to sense what we are in our life. When we simplify the situation, when we take away the externals and remove ourselves from the ringing phone, the television, the people who visit us, the dog who needs a walk, we get a chance—which is absolutely the most valuable thing there is—to face ourselves. Meditation is not about some state, but about the meditator. It's not about some activity, or about fixing something, or accomplishing something. It's about ourselves. If we don't simplify the situation the chance of taking a good look at ourselves is very small—because what we tend to look at isn't ourselves, but everything else. If something goes wrong, what do we look at? We look at what's going wrong, and usually at others we think have made it go wrong. We're looking *out there* all the time, and not at ourselves.

When I say meditation is about the meditator, I do not mean that we engage in self-analysis. That's not it either. So what do we do?

Once we have assumed our best posture (which should be balanced, easy), we just sit there, we do zazen. What do I mean by "just sit there"? It's the most demanding of all activities. Usually in meditation we don't shut our eyes. But right now I'd like you to shut your eyes and just *sit* there. What's going on? All sorts of things. A tiny twitch in your left shoulder; a pressure in your side . . . Notice your face for a moment. Feel it. Is it tense anywhere? Around the mouth, around the forehead? Now move down a bit. Notice your neck, just feel it. Then your shoulders, your back, chest, abdominal area, your arms, thighs. Keep feeling whatever you find. And feel your breath as it comes and goes. Don't try to control it, just feel it. Our first instinct is to try to control the breath. Just let your breath be as it is. It may be high in your chest, it may be in the middle, it may be low. It may feel tense. Just experience it as it is. Now just feel all of that. If a car goes by outside, hear it. If a plane flies over, notice that. You might hear a refrigerator going on and off. Just be that. That's all you have to do, absolutely all you have to do: experience that, and just stay with it. Now you can open your eyes.

If you can just do that for three minutes, that's miraculous. Usually after about a minute we begin to think. Our interest in just being with reality (which is what we have just done) is very low. "You mean that is all there is to zazen?" We don't like that. "We're seeking enlightenment, aren't we?" Our interest in reality is extremely low. No, we want to think. We want to worry through all of our preoccupations. We want to figure life out. And so before we know it we've forgotten all about this moment, and we've drifted off into thinking about something: our boyfriend, our girlfriend, our child, our boss, our current fear . . . off we go! There's nothing sinful about such fantasizing except that when we're lost in that, we've lost something else. When we're lost in thought, when we're dreaming, what have we lost? We've lost reality. Our life has escaped us. . . .

When we practice like this, we get acquainted with ourselves, how our lives work, what we are doing with them. If we find that certain thoughts come up hundreds of times, we know something about ourselves that we didn't know before. Perhaps we incessantly think about the past, or the future. Some people always think about events, some people always think about other people. Some people always think about themselves. Some people's thoughts are almost entirely judgments about other people. Until we have labeled for four or five years, we don't know ourselves very well.

When we label thoughts precisely and carefully, what happens to them? They begin to quiet down. We don't have to force ourselves to get rid of them. When they quiet down, we return to the experience of the body and the breath, over and over and over. I can't emphasize enough that we *don't* just do this three times, we do it ten thousand times; and as we do it, our life transforms. That's a theoretical description of sitting. It's very simple; there's nothing complicated about it.

# Gary Snyder

## *Just One Breath*

*The benefits of formal meditation are well documented, but
American poet Gary Snyder finds rewards in an interlude of only
one breath.*

IN THIS WORLD of onrushing events the act of meditation—even just a "one-breath" meditation—straight-
ening the back, clearing the mind for a moment—is a
refreshing island in the stream. Although the term *meditation*
has mystical and religious connotations for many people, it
is a simple and plain activity. Attention: deliberate stillness
and silence. As anyone who has practiced sitting knows, the
quieted mind has many paths, most of them tedious and
ordinary. Then, right in the midst of meditation, totally
unexpected images or feelings may sometimes erupt, and
there is a way into a vivid transparency. But whatever comes
up, sitting is always instructive. There is ample testimony
that a practice of meditation pursued over months and years
brings some degree of self-understanding, serenity, focus,
and self-confidence to the person who stays with it. There

is also a deep gratitude that one comes to feel for this world of beings, teachers, and teachings.

No one—guru or roshi or priest—can program for long what a person might think or feel in private reflection. We learn that we cannot in any literal sense control our mind. Meditation cannot serve an ideology. A meditation teacher can only help a student understand the phenomena that rise from his or her own inner world—after the fact—and give tips on directions to go. A meditation teacher can be a check or guide for the wayfarer to measure herself against, and like any experienced guide can give good warning of brushy paths and dead-end canyons from personal experience. The teacher provides questions, not answers. Within a traditional Buddhist framework of ethical values and psychological insight, the mind essentially reveals itself.

Meditation is not just a rest or retreat from the turmoil of the stream or the impurity of the world. It is a way of *being* the stream, so that one can be at home in both the white water and the eddies. Meditation may take one out of the world, but it also puts one totally into it. . . .

People often confuse meditation with prayer, devotion, or vision. They are not the same. Meditation as a practice does not address itself to a deity or present itself as an opportunity for revelation. This is not to say that people who are meditating do not occasionally think they have received a revelation or experienced visions. They do. But to those for whom meditation is their central practice, a vision or a revelation is seen as just another phenomenon of consciousness and as such is not to be taken as exceptional. The meditator would simply experience the ground of consciousness, and in doing so avoid excluding or excessively elevating any thought or feeling. To do this one must release all sense of the "I" as experiencer, even the "I" that might think it is privileged to communicate with the divine. It is in sensitive areas such as these that a teacher can be a great help. This is mostly a description of the Buddhist meditation tradition, which has hewed consistently to a nontheistic practice over the centuries.

# Venerable Henepola Gunaratana

## The Great Teacher

*While meditating, we are learning about ourselves, even while
releasing a sense of "I" as experiencer. This understanding, as Sri
Lankan Venerable Gunaratana points out, answers our first question—
"What Is Meditation?"—and leads to the personal transformation
that answers our next question, "Why Meditate?"*

MEDITATION IS CALLED the Great Teacher. It is
the cleansing crucible fire that works slowly through
understanding. The greater your understanding, the more
flexible and tolerant you can be. The greater your understanding, the more compassionate you can be. You become
like a perfect parent or an ideal teacher. You are ready to
forgive and forget. You feel love toward others because you
understand them. And you understand others because you
have understood yourself. You have looked deeply inside
and seen self-illusion and your own human failings. You have
seen your own humanity and learned to forgive and to love.
When you have learned compassion for yourself, compassion for others is automatic. An accomplished meditator has
achieved a profound understanding of life, and he inevitably
relates to the world with a deep and uncritical love.

Meditation is a lot like cultivating a new land. To make a field out of a forest, first you have to clear the trees and pull out the stumps. Then you till the soil and you fertilize it. Then you sow your seed and you harvest your crops. To cultivate your mind, first you have to clear out the various irritants that are in the way, pull them right out by the root so that they won't grow back. Then you fertilize. You pump energy and discipline into the mental soil. Then you sow the seed and you harvest your crops of faith, morality, mindfulness, and wisdom.

Faith and morality, by the way, have a special meaning in this context. Buddhism does not advocate faith in the sense of believing something because it is written in a book or attributed to a prophet or taught to you by some authority figure. The meaning here is closer to confidence. It is knowing that something is true because you have seen it work, because you have observed that very thing within yourself. In the same way, morality is not a ritualistic obedience to some exterior, imposed code of behavior. It is rather a healthy habit pattern which you have consciously and voluntarily chosen to impose upon yourself because you recognize its superiority to your present behavior.

The purpose of meditation is personal transformation. The you that goes in one side of the meditation experience is not the same you that comes out the other side. It changes your character by a process of sensitization, by making you deeply aware of your own thoughts, words, and deeds. Your arrogance evaporates and your antagonism dries up. Your mind becomes still and calm. And your life smooths out. Thus meditation properly performed prepares you to meet the ups and downs of existence. It reduces your tension, your fear, and your worry. Restlessness recedes, and passion moderates. Things begin to fall into place and your life becomes a glide instead of a struggle. All of this happens through understanding.

Meditation sharpens your concentration and your thinking power. Then, piece by piece, your own subconscious motives and mechanics become clear to you. Your intuition sharpens. The precision of your thought increases and gradually you come to a direct knowledge of things as they really are, without prejudice and without illusion. So is this reason enough to bother? Scarcely. These are just promises on paper. There is only one way you will ever know if meditation is worth the effort. Learn to do it right, and do it. See for yourself.

# Part II

# Why Meditate?

# The Buddha

## *The Greater Discourse on the Foundations of Mindfulness*

*From the time the Buddha began teaching, he was asked the question "Why meditate?" One of his earliest answers comes from his core teaching on the foundations of mindfulness, in which he told his monks that meditation led to the overcoming of pain and led to the realization of Nibbana (Nirvana). One morning, at Jeta's Grove in Savatthi, India, he further described the benefits of meditation to his own son, Rahula, who had become one of his disciples.*

"THERE IS, MONKS, this one way to the purification of beings, for the overcoming of sorrow and distress, for the disappearance of pain and sadness, for the gaining of the right path, for the realisation of Nibbana:—that is to say the four foundations of mindfulness."

# The Buddha

## The Greater Discourse of Advice to [His Son] Rahula

"RAHULA, DEVELOP MEDITATION that is like
. . . the earth; for when you develop meditation that
is like the earth, arisen agreeable and disagreeable contacts
will not invade your mind and remain. Just as people throw
clean things and dirty things, excrement, urine, spittle, pus,
and blood on the earth, and the earth is not horrified, humiliated, and disgusted because of that, so too, Rahula, develop meditation that is like the earth; for when you develop
meditation that is like the earth, arisen agreeable and disagreeable contacts will not invade your mind and remain.

"Rahula, develop meditation that is like water; for when
you develop meditation that is like water, arisen agreeable
and disagreeable contacts will not invade your mind and
remain. Just as people wash clean things and dirty things
. . . and the water is not horrified, humiliated, and dis-

gusted because of that, so too, Rahula, develop meditation that is like water; for when you develop meditation that is like water, arisen agreeable and disagreeable contacts will not invade your mind and remain.

"Rahula, develop meditation that is like fire; for when you develop meditation that is like fire, arisen agreeable and disagreeable contacts will not invade your mind and remain. Just as people burn clean things and dirty things . . . and the fire is not horrified, humiliated, and disgusted . . .

"Rahula, develop meditation that is like air; for when you develop meditation that is like air, arisen agreeable and disagreeable contacts will not invade your mind and remain. Just as the air blows on clean things and dirty things . . . and the air is not horrified, humiliated, and disgusted . . .

"Rahula, develop meditation that is like space; for when you develop meditation that is like space, arisen agreeable and disagreeable contacts will not invade your mind and remain. Just as space is not established anywhere, so too, Rahula, develop meditation that is like space; for when you develop meditation that is like space, arisen agreeable and disagreeable contacts will not invade your mind and remain.

"Rahula, develop meditation on loving-kindness; for when you develop meditation on loving-kindness, any ill will will be abandoned.

"Rahula, develop meditation on compassion; for when you develop meditation on compassion, any cruelty will be abandoned.

"Rahula, develop meditation on appreciative joy; for

when you develop meditation on appreciative joy, any discontent will be abandoned.

"Rahula, develop meditation on equanimity; for when you develop meditation on equanimity, any aversion will be abandoned.

"Rahula, develop meditation on foulness; for when you develop meditation on foulness, any lust will be abandoned.

"Rahula, develop meditation on the perception of impermanence; for when you develop meditation on the perception of impermanence, the conceit 'I am' will be abandoned. . . ."

# Thich Nhat Hanh

## *To Achieve Necessary Awareness*

*In the earliest days of the Buddha's teachings, people were curious
about why his disciples practiced as they did. Vietnamese Zen
teacher Thich Nhat Hanh describes the Buddha's encounter with
one questioner and outlines three answers to the question
"Why meditate?"*

I REMEMBER A SHORT conversation between the Buddha and a philosopher of his time.

"I have heard that Buddhism is a doctrine of enlightenment. What is your method? What do you practice every day?"

"We walk, we eat, we wash ourselves, we sit down."

"What is so special about that? Everyone walks, eats, washes, sits down."

"Sir, when we walk, we are aware that we are walking; when we eat, we are aware that we are eating. . . . When others walk, eat, wash, or sit down, they are generally not aware of what they are doing."

In Buddhism, mindfulness is the key. Mindfulness is the energy that sheds light on all things and all activities, producing the power of concentration, bringing forth deep insight and awakening. Mindfulness is at the base of all Buddhist practice.

*To shed light on all things?* This is the point of departure. If I live without mindfulness, in forgetfulness, I am, as Albert Camus says in his novel *The Stranger,* living "like a dead person." The ancient Zen masters used to say, "If we live in forgetfulness, we die in a dream." How many among us live "like a dead person"! The first thing we have to do is to return to life, to wake up and be mindful of each thing we do. Are we aware when we are eating, drinking, sitting in meditation? Or are we wasting our time, living in forgetfulness?

*To produce the power of concentration?* Mindfulness helps us focus our attention on and know what we are doing. Usually we are a prisoner of society. Our energies are dispersed here and there. Our body and our mind are not in harmony. To begin to be aware of what we are doing, saying, and thinking is to begin to resist the invasion by our surroundings and by all of our wrong perceptions. When the lamp of awareness is lit, our whole being lights up, and each passing thought and emotion is also lit up. Self-confidence is reestablished, the shadows of illusion no longer overwhelm us, and our concentration develops to its fullest. We wash our hands, dress, perform everyday actions as before, but now we are *aware* of our actions, words, and thoughts.

The practice of mindfulness is not only for novices. It is a lifelong practice for everyone, even the Buddha himself. The power of mindfulness and concentration is the spiritual force behind all of the great men and women of human history.

*To bring forth deep insight and awakening?* The aim of Zen Buddhism is a clear vision of reality, seeing things as they are, and that is acquired by the power of concentration. This clear vision is enlightenment. Enlightenment is always enlightenment about something. It is not abstract.

# Joseph Goldstein

## To Open, To Balance, To Explore

*The end of meditation practice may be the realization of enlightenment, but in the course of reaching that end, American Vipassana teacher Joseph Goldstein observes, meditators experience three benefits that justify the pursuit.*

A QUESTION THAT ARISES for beginners in meditation and also, at times, for people with years of experience, is "Why do we practice? Why are we doing this?" The effort and commitment needed to pursue meditation is so demanding that it is appropriate to ask what value it has and where it is leading.

Meditation has to do with opening what is closed in us, balancing what is reactive, and exploring and investigating what is hidden. That is the why of practice. We practice to open, to balance, and to explore.

## OPENING WHAT IS CLOSED

What is it that is closed in us? Our senses are closed, our bodies are closed. We spend so much of our time lost in thought, in judgment, in fantasy, and in daydreams that we do not pay careful attention to the direct experience of our senses—to sight and sound, to smell and taste, to sensations in the body. Because our attention is often scattered, perceptions through the sense doors become clouded. But as awareness and concentration become stronger through meditation, we spend less time lost in thought, and there is a much greater sensitivity and refinement in our sense impressions.

We also begin to open the body. Often there is not a free flow of energy in the body, and as we direct our awareness inward, we experience in a very clear and intimate way the accumulated tensions, knots, and holdings that are present. There are several different kinds of painful feelings that we might experience, and learning to distinguish and relate to these feelings of discomfort or pain is an important part of meditation practice, because it is one of the very first things that we open to as our practice develops.

One kind of pain that we might experience is that of a danger signal. When we put our hand in fire and it starts to hurt, there is a clear message saying, "Take your hand out." . . .

There is another kind of pain, which can be called "dharma pain." These are the painful sensations that have accumulated in the body, those tensions, knots, and holdings that we carry around all the time but are mostly unaware of because our minds are distracted. As we sit and pay attention and become more inwardly silent, there is a growing awareness of these painful feelings. This is, in fact, a sign of progress, because we are becoming aware of what is always there but usually below the threshold of our sensitivity. What we want to do in meditation is to open to this dharma pain, to experience what is actually present. . . .

Learning how to work with the painful sensations that arise in our practice is essential. It is a gateway to deeper levels of understanding, and the very fact that we can become aware of these painful feelings is itself a sign of stronger attention. As we approach this gateway of understanding, we don't want to turn away. We enter deeper levels by being soft and gentle and aware of what is happening. This is how we begin to fulfill the first aspect of practice: opening what is closed. And it is this openness to experience that is the foundation for the second aspect of practice: balancing what is reactive.

## BALANCING WHAT IS REACTIVE

What is it that is reactive? Our minds are reactive: liking and disliking, judging and comparing, clinging and con-

demning. Our minds are like a balance scale, and as long
as we're identified with these judgments and preferences,
likes and dislikes, wants and aversions, our minds are continually thrown out of balance, caught in a tiring whirlwind
of reactivity. It is through the power of mindfulness that we
can come to a place of balance and rest. Mindfulness is that
quality of attention which notices without choosing, without
preference; it is a choiceless awareness that, like the sun,
shines on all things equally. . . .

There is also a rhythm in our practice, an inner rhythm
to the breath, sensations, thoughts, emotions, feelings, images, and sounds. When we are nonreactive, when we open
and note just what's happening in each moment, without
holding on, without pushing away, without struggle, then
we find this inner rhythm. And when we experience this,
we begin to enjoy a certain ease and effortlessness in practice.

In order to find the rhythm, however, a great effort is
needed. It's the effort to pay attention, to bring the mind
into each moment. In the beginning the mind is scattered,
so we have to make an effort to contain and focus it. But
as we do this, moment after moment, at times everything
will click and we find the balance. It's like learning to ride
a bicycle; we will get on and pedal and at first are continually falling off one side or the other, until in one moment,
the sense of balance is established, and then it's easy. Meditation develops in the same way. It takes effort to be mindful in each moment so that the rhythm can be discovered.

In every moment of mindfulness, whatever the object is, whether it is the breath, sensations or sounds, thoughts or emotions, in every moment of simply noting and noticing what's there, there's no reactivity in the mind. There's no clinging and no condemning, just an accepting awareness of what's present. Every moment of mindfulness is helping to establish oneself in this inner balance and rhythm.

## EXPLORING WHAT IS HIDDEN

The third aspect of meditation is to investigate or reveal what is hidden. What is hidden is the true nature of our experience. The truth is what is hidden. One of the main ways the truth is camouflaged is through identification with and tendency to be lost in concepts. To a large extent, we confuse our ideas about things for the experience itself. A very essential part of meditation practice is going from the level of concept to the level of direct experience. . . .

Why is this so important? The distinction between our concepts and the reality of experience is crucial in terms of understanding where the practice is leading, because concepts cover what is true. The concepts we have of things remain the same. The names that we give to things don't change. My "knee" hurt yesterday, my "knee" hurts today, and it will probably hurt the next time I sit. Not only do we solidify the sense of "knee" through our concept, as if it were something more or less permanent, but this sense of its being static or permanent also makes it much easier for us to identify with it as being "I" or "mine." Now, not only is there a "knee" that hurts, it is "my knee."

When we come to what is truly happening, however, we see that the experience is changing every instant. Things do not stay the same even for two moments. What we are conceiving of as "my knee" is in the reality of direct experience a mass of instantaneously changing sensations, with no solidity or permanence at all. But as long as we stay on the concept level, we are unable to see or understand this momentary nature of phenomena.

Our meditation begins to investigate what is hidden. We go from the *level* of concept to the level of direct experience, whether it's bodily sensations or sight or sound or smell or taste; we begin to experience the nature and process of thoughts and emotions, rather than being identified with their contents. As we connect with what we are experiencing in each moment, we begin to discover some things that may have been previously hidden or obscure.

First, we discover that everything is changing, that everything we thought was solid, unchanging, or permanent is in a state of flux. People may hear this and think, "I know that everything is impermanent. It doesn't sound so startling to me." It's true that we know it intellectually, but we don't know it deeply, viscerally; we don't know it from the inside out. Meditation is a vehicle for opening to the truth of this impermanence on deeper and deeper levels. Every sensation, every thought, every feeling, every sound, every taste—*everything*—inside and outside, is in a state of continual dissolution.

When we see that, when we really know it, that understanding deconditions grasping in the mind, deconditions our attachments. Have you ever gone to a stream and tried to grasp a bubble in the water with the hope of holding on to it? Probably not, because you clearly know that it's just a bubble, arising and dissolving. Everything is like that. It is possible to see this, to experience it in a deeply integrated way. When we develop this clarity of vision and understanding, then the mind is much less inclined to grasp, because we see that there is nothing to hold on to. And as we are less attached, less grasping, less clinging, there is also less suffering in our lives.

As we see the impermanence of things, we also begin to understand the truth of the basic insecurity about all phenomena. Things are insecure or unsatisfactory in the sense that something that is always changing is incapable of giving us a lasting sense of completion or fulfillment. When we see this deeply in ourselves, it also begins to decondition the strong forces of desire and grasping in the mind. We begin to let go, allowing for the inevitable flow of change, rather than trying to hold on to something, thinking that it will make us happy forever after.

We see the impermanence, we see the insecurity. And we begin to understand what is the unique jewel of the Buddha's enlightenment—insight into the selflessness of the whole process of mind and body, understanding that there is no one behind it to whom it is happening. There is no one to whom this changing process belongs, there is no owner of it. This is a subtle and radical transformation of our normal way of understanding, and it develops into a deep wisdom as we go from the level of concept to the level of direct experience. When we understand in a very intuitive and connected way the essential insubstantiality, emptiness, and selflessness of phenomena, we begin to weaken the fundamental attachment we have to the sense of "I," of "self," of "me," of "mine," those concepts around which our whole lives have revolved. We see that this "I" is an illusion, a concept that we've created, and we start the journey of integrating the possibility of greater freedom in our lives.

It's only by paying careful attention in each moment to what is true, not to our ideas about it, but to what is actually there, that we are able to know for ourselves in a deeply transforming way the impermanence, insecurity, and selflessness that characterize all our experience.

# Joseph Goldstein

## *Exercise / Concepts and Reality*

ONE OF THE most important aspects of meditation practice is going from the level of concept
to the level of direct experience. In order to understand this more fully, sit quietly for a few moments,
letting one hand rest lightly on the other. What do
you experience? Perhaps there is the thought "I experience my hands or fingers touching." There might
be a mental image or picture of hands as they rest on
your lap. There may also be the awareness of different
sensations such as pressure, warmth, and tingling. If
you can feel quite precisely and accurately the sensations that are present in this moment of awareness,
what happens to the thought or image of "hand"? You
might try doing this exercise with closed eyes. Please

take some time to investigate and distinguish these different levels of experience.

When you walk, what are you aware of in each step? Is there an image of the form of the foot or leg? Can you feel the different sensations in the movement? What are they? What happens to the image as you feel the sensations? What happens to the sensations themselves?

Both in times of formal practice and everyday life, practice distinguishing the level of concept from the level of bare experience.

# Ayya Khema

## To Transcend Everyday Consciousness

*To move from the level of concept to the level of bare experience, it
is necessary, notes German-born Theravadan nun and teacher Ayya
Khema, to transcend our everyday consciousness.*

THERE IS VERY little doubt that those of us who want
to meditate are looking for something other than what
we are used to in the world. We are already wise enough
to know that the world hasn't fulfilled our expectations and
maybe we already know that it will never do so. That is a
big step in itself.

When we sit down to meditate, we are trying to transcend our everyday consciousness: the one with which we
transact our ordinary business, the one used in the world's
marketplace as we go shopping, bring up our children, work
in an office or in our business, clean the house, check our
bank statements, and all the rest of daily living. That kind
of consciousness is known to everyone and without it we
can't function. It is our survival consciousness and we need
it for that. It cannot reach far enough or deep enough into

the Buddha's teachings, because these are unique and profound; our everyday consciousness is neither unique nor
profound, it's just utilitarian.

In order to attain the kind of consciousness that is capable
of going deeply enough into the teachings to make them
our own and thereby change our whole inner view, we need
a mind with the ability to remove itself from the ordinary
thinking process. That is only possible through meditation.
There is no other way. Meditation is therefore a means and
not an end in itself. It is a means to change the mind's
capacity in such a way that we can see entirely different
realities from the ones we are used to. The recognition that
meditation is a tool is important, because it is often wrongly
considered to be an end in itself. In Pali it is called *bhavana,*
"mind training," to be used for honing the mind until it
becomes such a sharp tool that it cuts through everyday
realities.

Most people sit down to meditate to get some peace and
quiet into their minds, which is as good a reason as any
other; however, that is not the purpose of meditation but
rather one essential aspect of it. Calm and insight (*samatha*
and *vipassana*) are the only two directions in meditation.
There are many methods. The Buddha taught, according to
the Pali canon, forty different methods. We do not need to
practice that many. Some of the forty methods are strictly
insight methods. Some are used only to attain calm. The
goal of meditation is insight, and tranquillity the means.

Everybody is looking for some calm, some peace, to be

able to stop the mind from continuing its usual chatter. While it is necessary to cultivate the calm aspect of meditation, most people find it impossible to sit down and immediately become tranquil. Unfortunately our minds are used to being exactly the opposite. They are thinking, evaluating and judging from morning to night and then dreaming from night to morning, so that they don't get a moment's rest. If we were to treat our bodies in that way we would soon be out of commission. The body can't handle that for more than a few days, never having a moment's rest, working all the time. When we ask this of our mind we are surprised that things don't turn out the way we hoped and that the world doesn't work the way we thought it would. It would be even more surprising if it were otherwise, because what we see in our own mind is exactly what is going on in everybody else's. That too is an important aspect of the meditative mind, to realize that we are not individually burdened with all this unsatisfactoriness *(dukkha)*. It is a universal aspect of existence, comprising the first Noble Truth of the Buddha's teaching.

*Dukkha* is universal. It doesn't belong to any one of us. We have no monopoly. Because our minds are not yet trained, the world is the way it is and meditation is a struggle. We need to learn to halt the habit patterns of the mind. Our minds are used to thinking, but when we want to become calm and peaceful that is exactly what we have to stop doing. It is easier said than done, because the mind will continue to do what it is used to doing. There is another reason why it finds it difficult to refrain from its habits: thinking is the only ego support we have while we are meditating, and particularly when we keep noble silence. "I think, therefore I am." Western philosophy accepts that as an absolute. Actually it is a relative truth, which all of us experience.

When we are thinking, we know that we are here; when there is no chattering in the mind, we believe we lose control. It's exactly the other way around. As long as we can't stop thinking, we have no control. We are in control of our mind only when we are able to stop thinking when we want to. The difficulty arising for most, if not all, meditators is this aspect of letting go. To let go of the only ego support we have while we are meditating, namely our thinking, has to be a deliberate act. When we go about our daily business, we deliberately direct our mind towards what we want to do. If we want to work in the kitchen, we deliberately go there and turn our attention to what needs to be done. If we have work to do in an office, we deliberately turn our mind to letters, files and other office business. It's the same in meditation.

Our first difficulty is that although we would like to become peaceful and calm and have no thoughts, our mind does not want to obey. It refuses to do so because then we would appear to have no support for our existence, and because our habits are against it. So instead of trying over and over again to become calm we can use whatever arises to gain some insight. A little bit of insight brings a little bit of calm, and a little bit of calm brings a little bit of insight. Calm has no other purpose than to change our ordinary, everyday consciousness to a transcendental consciousness, which is able to understand and use the teachings of the Buddha to change from an ordinary being into a transcendental being. If calm doesn't arise it is not a great problem, because whatever else does arise helps us to gain some insight into who we really are. . . .

Meditation is the means by which we can practice mindfulness to the point where insight becomes so strong that we can see absolute reality behind the relative. Mindfulness trained in meditation can then continue in every activity. At the moment we are only considering mindfulness of body action, because we can make use of it constantly. As the body can be touched and seen, we have a chance of really having mind and body in the same place, instead of the mind running off into its usual ramifications and the body doing something else. If we were to keep mind and body in one place we would have no problem in watching the breath, because that is all that is really happening; we are breathing. Nothing else. Everything else is conjecture. . . .

Only people who never meditate believe what they are thinking. When one has labeled one's thoughts in meditation one realizes that the thinking process is quite arbitrary, and often has no real meaning; nonsense, "no sense" in it, and not even wanted.

Gaining such an insight into our thinking during meditation helps us in everyday life to drop thoughts which are not useful, and that makes our life less stressful. If we can drop a thought by labeling it during meditation we can do the same in daily life. Otherwise we have meditated in vain—we have been sitting and getting a knee pain without any result. We must be able to transfer our meditation practice into everyday life.

In meditation we drop all thoughts. When they recur, we drop them again. We substitute for them by putting our attention on the breath. In daily life we drop unwholesome thoughts and substitute wholesome ones. It's exactly the same substitution process, and when we have learned it in meditation it can become a good habit in daily life. Not that it will always work (there's no such thing as "always"), but we understand the possibilities.

When we listen to the words of the Buddha, we know that he is showing us an ideal to work for, and that if we have not yet reached that ideal we need not blame our-selves. "Awareness, no blame, change" is an important for-mula to remember: to become aware of what is going on within oneself but not to attach any blame to it. Things are the way they are, but we, as thinking human beings, have the ability to change and that is what we are doing in med-itation.

# The Dhammapada

## The Mind

*What happens when one does or doesn't meditate is addressed in*
*The Dhammapada. According to Theravadan tradition, these*
*verses were composed, in Pali, by the Buddha in response to*
*situations he encountered during his years of teaching.*

JUST AS AN arrow-maker straightens an arrow shaft, even
so the discerning man straightens his mind—so fickle and
unsteady, so difficult to guard and control.

As a fish when pulled out of water and cast on land throbs
and quivers, even so is this mind agitated. Hence one should
leave the realm of Māra.

Wonderful, indeed, it is to subdue the mind, so difficult
to subdue, ever swift, and wandering wherever it desires.
A tamed mind brings happiness.

Let the discerning man guard his mind, so difficult to
detect and extremely subtle, seizing whatever it desires. A
guarded mind brings happiness.

Dwelling in the cave (of the heart), without form, the
mind wanders far and moves alone. Those who subdue this

mind are liberated from the bonds of *Mara* [overwhelming passions].

When one's mind is not steadfast, when one knows not the Good Teaching and one's faith wavers, one's wisdom will not be perfected. . . .

Whatever harm an enemy may do to an enemy, or a hater to a hater, an ill-directed mind inflicts on oneself a greater harm.

# B. Alan Wallace

## To Investigate Reality

*An ill-directed mind can only be redirected by the cultivation of
ethical principles and spiritual practice, which Tibetan Buddhist
scholar B. Alan Wallace sees leading to meditative quiescence. This
tranquillity in turn leads to greater sanity, serenity, stability,
and clarity.*

SUPPOSE THAT EACH of us wore a device that picked
up all our thoughts, even the most subtle, unintentional
ones, and immediately blared them out through loudspeak-
ers strapped to the tops of our heads. As long as these
thoughts remain hidden, often even from ourselves, we are
able to present a fine semblance of sanity to those around
us. But for most of us this veneer would swiftly vanish if
others could hear the chaotic turbulence of our minds.

The whole of spiritual practice can be seen as cultivation
of deeper and deeper sanity. In Buddhism this path of making the mind sane is a gradual one, beginning with relatively
easy practices that bring about obvious, tangible benefits.
The first stage of practice is ethical discipline. . . . The direct, manifest result of a life focused on these ethical principles is a greater state of well-being for ourselves and for

those around us. Even without deep study or meditation, this brings about greater sanity and contentment.

As a result of this foundation of spiritual practice, our thoughts will be more wholesome, but our minds may still be scattered, unstable, and unclear. It is helpful to reinforce this foundation further by stabilizing our minds in meditation. In Buddhism the result of this practice is called *meditative quiescence, or tranquillity*. One contemplative of the Kagyupa order of Tibetan Buddhism sums up tranquillity practice as follows: "Tranquillity is achieved by focusing the mind on an object and maintaining it in that state until finally it is channeled into one stream of attention and evenness."

Thus, in the Buddhist context, meditative quiescence means more than just a peaceful feeling. It is a quality of awareness that is stable and vivid, clearly focused upon its chosen object. It is not an end in itself, but a fine tool to be employed in the third phase of traditional Buddhist practice, namely, insight. The same author says of insight practice: "Insight is attained through a general and detailed examination of reality and the systematic application of intellectual discrimination."

Experiential insight into the nature of reality is the direct antidote to ignorance, the mental affliction that lies at the root of all distortions of the mind, unwholesome behavior, and suffering. However, without achieving meditative quiescence, the healing power of insight is limited, and ignorance cannot be fully dispelled. . . .

Certainly it is possible to gain some degree of insight without having achieved great mental stability, but such illumination is like the light of a candle flickering in a breeze. This insight may be very meaningful, but due to the lack of meditative quiescence, it is fleeting, and difficult for the meditator to experience repeatedly.

Just as it is possible to acquire a limited degree of insight without meditative quiescence, so one may experience compassion to some extent without insight. But the most profound spiritual awakening occurs upon the foundation of all three—meditative quiescence, insight, and compassion— and it is for this purpose that one cultivates meditative quiescence. . . .

When we finally attain meditative quiescence, we are free of even the subtle forms of excitement and laxity. During the early phases of practice, considerable degrees of effort are required, but as we progress, more and more subtle effort suffices. Gradually the meditation becomes effortless, and we can sustain each session for hours on end.

Benefits from this practice are also evident between formal meditation sessions. The mind becomes so refined and stable that it is very difficult for mental distortions to arise. And even when they do occur, they are relatively impotent and short-lived. Through the attainment of meditative quiescence, the mind is brought to such a state of heightened sanity it is very difficult for these afflictions to thrive. In addition, one will experience an unprecedented quality of inner well-being that arises from the balance and health of the mind. Due to the shifts in the energies experienced in the body (closely related to the nervous system), one will experience a delightful sense of physical lightness and buoyancy. . . .

In Buddhist practice the chief purpose of attaining meditative quiescence is to use this refined state of awareness for investigating the nature of reality. Meditative quiescence by itself is a temporary achievement that can easily be lost, especially if one becomes immersed once again in a hectic, turbulent way of life. Only by using the mind that has been trained in meditative quiescence is it possible to gain the depth of insight needed to utterly uproot the fundamental distortions of the mind, which are the root of suffering.

In the meantime, the cultivation of meditative quiescence is something that brings us greater sanity, serenity, stability, and clarity. This is bound to aid us in all the pursuits worthy of our precious lives.

# Jack Kornfield

## To Heal the Body, Heart, and Mind

*American Vipassana teacher Jack Kornfield observes that the pursuit of meditative quiescence heals not only our minds but our bodies and hearts as well.*

### HEALING THE BODY

MEDITATION PRACTICE OFTEN begins with techniques for bringing us to an awareness of our bodies. This is especially important in a culture such as ours, which has neglected physical and instinctual life. James Joyce wrote of one character, "Mr. Duffy lived a short distance from his body." So many of us do. In meditation, we can slow down and sit quietly, truly staying with whatever arises. With awareness, we can cultivate a willingness to open to physical experiences without struggling against them, to actually live in our bodies. As we do so, we feel more clearly its pleasures and its pains. Because our acculturation teaches us to avoid or run from pain, we do not know much about it. To heal the body we must study pain. When we bring close attention to our physical pains, we will notice several kinds. We see that sometimes pain arises as we adjust to an unaccustomed sitting posture. Other times, pains arise as signals that we're sick or have a genuine physical problem. These pains call for a direct response and healing action from us.

However, most often the kinds of pains we encounter in meditative attention are not indications of physical problems. They are the painful, physical manifestations of our emotional, psychological, and spiritual holdings and contractions. Reich called these pains our muscular armor, the areas of our body that we have tightened over and over in painful situations as a way to protect ourselves from life's inevitable difficulties. Even a healthy person who sits somewhat comfortably to meditate will probably become aware of pains in his or her body. As we sit still, our shoulders, our backs, our jaws, or our necks may hurt. Accumulated knots in the fabric of our body, previously undetected, begin to reveal themselves as we open. As we become conscious of the pain they have held, we may also notice feelings, memories, or images connected specifically to each area of tension.

As we gradually include in our awareness all that we have previously shut out and neglected, our body heals. Learning to work with this opening is part of the art of meditation. We can bring an open and respectful attention to the sensations that make up our bodily experience. In this process, we must work to develop a feeling awareness of what is actually going on in the body. We can direct our attention to notice the patterns of our breathing, our posture, the way we hold our back, our chest, our belly, our pelvis. In all these areas we can carefully sense the free movement of energy or the contraction and holding that prevents it. . . .

## HEALING THE HEART

Just as we open and heal the body by sensing its rhythms and touching it with a deep and kind attention, so we can open and heal other dimensions of our being. The heart and the feelings go through a similar process of healing through the offering of our attention to their rhythms, nature, and needs. Most often, opening the heart begins by opening to a lifetime's accumulation of unacknowledged sorrow, both our personal sorrows and the universal sorrows of warfare, hunger, old age, illness, and death. At times we may experience this sorrow physically, as contractions and barriers around our heart, but more often we feel the depth of our wounds, our abandonment, our pain, as unshed tears. The Buddhists describe this as an ocean of human tears larger than the four great oceans.

As we . . . develop a meditative attention, the heart presents itself naturally for healing. The grief we have carried for so long, from pains and dashed expectations and hopes, arises.

## HEALING THE MIND

Just as we heal the body and the heart through awareness, so can we heal the mind. Just as we learn about the nature and rhythm of sensations and feelings, so can we learn about the nature of thoughts. As we notice our thoughts in meditation, we discover that they are not in our control—we swim in an uninvited constant stream of memories, plans, expectations, judgments, regrets. The mind begins to show how it contains all possibilities, often in conflict with one another—the beautiful qualities of a saint and the dark forces of a dictator and murderer. Out of these, the mind plans and imagines, creating endless struggles and scenarios for changing the world.

Yet the very root of these movements of mind is dissatisfaction. We seem to want both endless excitement and perfect peace. Instead of being served by our thinking, we are driven by it in many unconscious and unexamined ways. While thoughts can be enormously useful and creative, most often they dominate our experience with ideas of likes versus dislikes, higher versus lower, self versus other. They tell stories about our successes and failures, plan our security, habitually remind us of who and what we think we are.

This dualistic nature of thought is a root of our suffering. Whenever we think of ourselves as separate, fear and attachment arise and we grow constricted, defensive, ambitious, and territorial. To protect the separate self, we push certain things away, while to bolster it we hold on to other things and identify with them. . . .

Healing the mind takes place in two ways: In the first, we bring attention to the content of our thoughts and learn to redirect them more skillfully through practices of wise reflection. Through mindfulness, we can come to know and reduce the patterns of unhelpful worry and obsession, we can clarify our confusion and release destructive views and opinions. We can use conscious thought to reflect more deeply on what we value. Asking the question, Do I love well? . . . is an example of this, and we can also direct our thought into the skillful avenues of loving-kindness, respect, and ease of mind. Many Buddhist practices use the repetition of certain phrases in order to break through old, destructively repetitious patterns of thought to effect change.

However, even though we work to reeducate the mind, we can never be completely successful. The mind seems to have a will of its own no matter how much we wish to direct it. So, for a deeper healing of the conflicts of the mind, we need to let go of our identification with them. To heal, we must learn to step back from all the stories of the mind, for the conflicts and opinions of our thoughts never end. As the Buddha said, "People with opinions just go around bothering one another." When we see that the mind's very nature is to think, to divide, to plan, we can release ourselves from its iron grip of separatism and come to rest in the body and heart. In this way, we step out of our identification, out of our expectations, opinions, and judgments and the conflicts to which they give rise. The mind thinks of the self as separate; the heart knows better. As one great Indian master, Sri Nisargadatta, put it, "The mind creates the abyss, and the heart crosses it."

Many of the great sorrows of the world arise when the mind is disconnected from the heart. In meditation we can reconnect with our heart and discover an inner sense of spaciousness, unity, and compassion underneath all the conflicts of thought. The heart allows for the stories and ideas, the fantasies and fears of the mind without believing in them, without having to follow them or having to fulfill them. When we touch beneath all the busyness of thought, we discover a sweet, healing silence, an inherent peacefulness in each of us, a goodness of heart, strength, and wholeness that is our birthright. This basic goodness is sometimes called our original nature, or Buddha nature. When we return to our original nature, when we see all the ways of the mind and yet rest in this peace and goodness, we discover the healing of the mind.

# Jon Kabat-Zinn

## To Pursue Your Vision

*All of the reasons why we meditate, according to Jon Kabat-Zinn, must be integrated into a vision of what we want our practice to be—a vision that underlies and sustains our ability to maintain our practice.*

IT IS VIRTUALLY impossible, and senseless anyway, to commit yourself to a daily meditation practice without some view of why you are doing it, what its value might be in your life, a sense of why this might be your way and not just another tilting at imaginary windmills. In traditional societies, this vision was supplied and continually reinforced by the culture. If you were a Buddhist, you might practice because the whole culture valued meditation as the path to clarity, compassion, and Buddhahood, a path of wisdom leading to the eradication of suffering. But in the Western cultural mainstream, you will find precious little support for choosing such a personal path of discipline and constancy, especially such an unusual one involving effort but non-doing, energy but no tangible "product." What's more, any superficial or romantic notions we might harbor of becoming a better person—more calm or more clear or more compassionate—don't endure for long when we face the turbulence of our lives, or even the prospect of getting up early in the morning when it is cold and dark to sit by yourself and be in the present moment. It's too easily put off or seen as trivial or of secondary importance, so it can always wait while you catch a little more sleep or at least stay warm in bed.

If you hope to bring meditation into your life in any kind of long-term, committed way, you will need a vision that is truly your own—one that is deep and tenacious and that lies close to the core of who you believe yourself to be, what you value in your life, and where you see yourself going. Only the strength of such a dynamic vision and the motivation from which it springs can possibly keep you on this path year in and year out, with a willingness to practice every day and to bring mindfulness to bear on whatever is happening, to open to whatever is perceived, and to let it point to where the holding is and where the letting go and the growing need to happen.

Meditation practice is hardly romantic. The ways in which we need to grow are usually those we are the most supremely defended against and are least willing to admit even exist, let alone take an undefended, mindful peek at and then action to change. It won't be sustaining enough to have a quixotic idea of yourself as a meditator, or to hold the opinion that meditation is good for you because it has been good for others, or because Eastern wisdom sounds deep to you, or because you are in the habit of meditating. The vision we are speaking of has to be renewed every day, has to be right out front all the time, because mindfulness itself requires this level of awareness of purpose, of intention. Otherwise, we might as well stay in bed.

The practice itself has to become the daily embodiment of your vision and contain what you value most deeply. It doesn't mean trying to change or be different from how you are, calm when you're not feeling calm, or kind when you really feel angry. Rather, it is bearing in mind what is most important to you so that it is not lost or betrayed in the heat and reactivity of a particular moment. If mindfulness is deeply important to you, then every moment is an opportunity to practice. . . .

Our vision has to do with our values, and with our personal blueprint for what is most important in life. It has to do with first principles. If you believe in love, do you manifest it or just talk a lot? If you believe in compassion, in non-harming, in kindness, in wisdom, in generosity, in calmness, in solitude, in non-doing, in being even-handed and clear, do you manifest these qualities in your daily life? This is the level of intentionality which is required to keep your meditation practice vital, so that it doesn't succumb to becoming purely a mechanical exercise, driven only by the forces of habit or belief.

# Shunryu Suzuki

## For Enlightenment

*Throughout Shunryu Suzuki's teachings, the Zen master stressed the*
*importance of maintaining practice. Because the Buddha nature*
*exists in each of us, from the time that we start zazen (Zen*
*meditative practice), there is enlightenment in our practice.*

A S A PHILOSOPHY, Buddhism is a very deep, wide, and firm system of thought, but Zen is not concerned about philosophical understanding. We emphasize practice. We should understand why our physical posture and breathing exercise are so important. Instead of having a deep understanding of the teaching, we need a strong confidence in our teaching, which says that originally we have Buddha nature. Our practice is based on this faith. . . .

Before Bodhidharma, people thought that after a long preparation, sudden enlightenment would come. Thus Zen practice was a kind of training to gain enlightenment. Actually, many people today are practicing zazen with this idea. But this is not the traditional understanding of Zen. The understanding passed down from Buddha to our time is that when you start zazen, there is enlightenment—even without any preparation. Whether you practice zazen or not, you have Buddha nature. Because you have it, there is enlightenment in your practice. The points we emphasize are not the stage we attain, but the strong confidence we have in our original nature and the sincerity of our practice. We should practice Zen with the same sincerity as Buddha. If originally we have Buddha nature, the reason we practice zazen is that we must behave like Buddha. To transmit our way is to transmit our spirit from Buddha. So we have to harmonize our spirit, our physical posture, and our activity with the traditional way.

*Part III*

# How to Meditate

# The Buddha

## The Greater Discourse on the Foundations of Mindfulness

*The Buddha's instructions about how to meditate were quite clear*
*and simple: go sit under a tree, cross your legs, and establish*
*mindfulness. Because what is simple is not always what is easy,*
*we'll look first at some general instructions on how to meditate,*
*then look more closely at posture, breath as an object, other forms*
*of meditation in everyday life, and some of the common problems*
*meditators encounter.*

"HERE A BHIKKHU [monk], gone to the forest or to the root of a tree or to an empty hut, sits down; having folded his legs crosswise, set his body erect, and established mindfulness in front of him . . ."

# Jack Kornfield

## Establishing a Daily Meditation Practice

*The ability for our mind and body to work together so that we never leave reality can be achieved only through daily practice. American Vipassana teacher Jack Kornfield compares establishing this daily practice to training a puppy.*

FIRST SELECT A suitable space for your regular meditation. It can be wherever you can sit easily with minimal disturbance: a corner of your bedroom or any other quiet spot in your home. Place a meditation cushion or chair there for your use. Arrange what is around so that you are reminded of your meditative purpose, so that it feels like a sacred and peaceful space. You may wish to make a simple altar with a flower or sacred image, or place your favorite spiritual books there for a few moments of inspiring reading. Let yourself enjoy creating this space for yourself.

Then select a regular time for practice that suits your schedule and temperament. If you are a morning person, experiment with a sitting before breakfast. If evening fits your temperament or schedule better, try that first. Begin with sitting ten or twenty minutes at a time. Later you can sit longer or more frequently. Daily meditation can become like bathing or toothbrushing. It can bring a regular cleansing and calming to your heart and mind.

Find a posture on the chair or cushion in which you can easily sit erect without being rigid. Let your body be firmly planted on the earth, your hands resting easily, your heart soft, your eyes closed gently. At first feel your body and consciously soften any obvious tension. Let go of any habitual thoughts or plans. Bring your attention to feel the sensations of your breathing. Take a few deep breaths to sense where you can feel the breath most easily, as coolness or tingling in the nostrils or throat, as movement of the chest, or rise and fall of the belly. Then let your breath be natural. Feel the sensations of your natural breathing very carefully, relaxing into each breath as you feel it, noticing how the soft sensations of breathing come and go with the changing breath.

After a few breaths your mind will probably wander. When you notice this, no matter how long or short a time you have been away, simply come back to the next breath. Before you return, you can mindfully acknowledge where you have gone with a soft word in the back of your mind, such as "thinking," "wandering," "hearing," "itching." After softly and silently naming to yourself where your attention has been, gently and directly return to feel the next breath. Later on in your meditation you will be able to work with the places your mind wanders to, but for initial training, one word of acknowledgment and a simple return to the breath is best.

As you sit, let the breath change rhythms naturally, allowing it to be short, long, fast, slow, rough, or easy. Calm yourself by relaxing into the breath. When your breath becomes soft, let your attention become gentle and careful, as soft as the breath itself.

Like training a puppy, gently bring yourself back a thousand times. Over weeks and months of this practice you will gradually learn to calm and center yourself using the breath. There will be many cycles in this process, stormy days alternating with clear days. Just stay with it. As you do, listening deeply, you will find the breath helping to connect and quiet your whole body and mind.

Working with the breath is an excellent foundation for the other meditations presented in this book. After developing some calm and skills, and connecting with your breath, you can then extend your range of meditation to include healing and awareness of all the levels of your body and mind. You will discover how awareness of your breath can serve as a steady basis for all you do.

# Zen Master Dogen

## Zen Meditation Instructions

*With the general explanation of meditation and a daily practice in mind, it's time to actually sit down and begin. First, thirteenth-century Zen master Dogen, then the Dalai Lama, then Vipassana teacher Joseph Goldstein give us specific instructions.*

FOR INTENSIVE ZEN meditation, a quiet room is appropriate. Food and drink are to be moderate. Letting go of all mental objects, taking a respite from all concerns, not thinking of good or evil, not being concerned with right or wrong, halt the operations of mind, intellect, and consciousness, stop assessment by thought, imagination, and view. Do not aim to become a Buddha, and how could it be limited to sitting or reclining?

Spread a thick sitting mat where you usually sit, and use a cushion on top of this. You may sit in the full-lotus posture, or in the half-lotus posture. For the full-lotus posture, first place the right foot on the left thigh, then the left foot on the right thigh. For the half-lotus posture, just place the left foot on the right thigh. Wear loose clothing, and keep it orderly.

Next place the right hand on the left leg, and the left hand on the right hand, with palms facing upward. The two thumbs face each other and hold each other up.

Now sit upright, with your body straight. Do not lean to the left or tilt to the right, bend forward or lean backward. Align the ears with the shoulders, and the nose with the navel. The tongue should rest on the upper palate, the teeth and lips should be closed. The eyes should always be open.

The breathing passes subtly through the nose.

Once the physical form is in order, exhale fully through the mouth once, sway left and right, then settle into sitting perfectly still.

Think of what does not think. How do you think of what does not think? It is not thinking.

This is the essential art of sitting Zen meditation.

# The Dalai Lama

## Tibetan Meditation Instructions

Irst, look to your posture: arrange the legs in the
most comfortable position; set the backbone as straight
as an arrow. Place your hands in the position of meditative
equipoise, four finger widths below the navel, with the left
hand on the bottom, right hand on top, and your thumbs
touching to form a triangle. This placement of the hands
has connection with the place inside the body where inner
heat is generated. Bending the neck down slightly, allow the
mouth and teeth to be as usual, with the top of the tongue
touching the roof of the mouth near the top teeth. Let the
eyes gaze downwards loosely—it is not necessary that they
be directed to the end of the nose; they can be pointed
toward the floor in front of you if this seems more natural.
Do not open the eyes too wide nor forcefully close them;
leave them open a little. Sometimes they will close of their

own accord; that is all right. Even if your eyes are open, when your mental consciousness becomes steady upon its object, these appearances to the eye consciousness will not disturb you.

For those of you who wear eyeglasses, have you noticed that when you take off your glasses, because of the unclarity there is less danger from the generation of excitement and more danger of laxity? Do you find that there is a difference between facing and not facing the wall? When you face the wall, you may find that there is less danger of excitement or scattering. These kinds of things can be determined through your own experience. . . .

Try to leave your mind vividly in a natural state, without thinking of what happened in the past or of what you are planning for the future, without generating any conceptuality. Where does it seem that your consciousness is? Is it with the eyes or where is it? Most likely you have a sense that it is associated with the eyes since we derive most of our awareness of the world through vision. This is due to having relied too much on our sense consciousness. However, the existence of a separate mental consciousness can be ascertained; for example, when attention is diverted by sound, that which appears to the eye consciousness is not noticed. This indicates that a separate mental consciousness is paying more attention to sound heard by the ear consciousness than to the perceptions of the eye consciousness.

With persistent practice, consciousness may eventually be perceived or felt as an entity of mere luminosity and knowing, to which anything is capable of appearing and which, when appropriate conditions arise, can be generated in the image of whatsoever object. As long as the mind does not encounter the external circumstance of conceptuality, it will abide empty without anything appearing in it, like clear water. Its very entity is that of mere experience. Let the mind flow of its own accord without conceptual overlay. Let the mind rest in its natural state, and observe it. In the beginning, when you are not used to this practice, it is quite difficult, but in time the mind appears like clear water. Then, stay with this unfabricated mind without allowing conceptions to be generated. In realizing this nature of the mind, we have for the first time located the object of observation of this internal type of meditation.

The best time for practicing this form of meditation is in the morning, in a quiet place, when the mind is very clear and alert. It helps not to have eaten too much the night before nor to sleep too much; this makes the mind lighter and sharper the next morning. Gradually the mind will become more and more stable; mindfulness and memory will become clearer.

# Joseph Goldstein

## *Vipassana Meditation Instructions*

SIT COMFORTABLY, WITH your back straight but not stiff or tense. Gently close your eyes and feel the sensations of the breath as the air passes the nostrils or upper lip. The sensations of the in-breath appear simply and naturally. Notice how the out-breath appears. Or you might choose to feel the movement of your chest or abdomen as the breath enters and leaves your body.

Wherever you choose to follow the sensations of breathing, whether the in and out at the nostrils or the movement of the chest or abdomen, train your awareness to connect clearly with the first moment of the beginning in-breath. Then sustain the attention for the duration of just that one in-coming breath. Connect again at the beginning of the out-breath and sustain your attention till the end.

It is important not to become overly ambitious. We all

have the capacity to feel one breath completely. But if we try to do more than that, if we have the idea that we are going to be mindful of our breathing for half an hour, then that is much too much. To sustain unbroken attention for that amount of time is far beyond the capacity of our mind, and so we quickly become discouraged. Connect and sustain for just one breath . . . and then one more. In this way you can work well within your capacity, and your mind will begin to concentrate simply and easily.

At times other objects will arise—physical sensations, thoughts, images, emotions. Notice how all these appearances arise and change in the open awareness of mind. Often we become distracted, lost in the display of experience, no longer mindful. As soon as you remember, come back to the simple state of awareness.

It can be helpful in the beginning to focus primarily, although not exclusively, on the breath. Focusing in this way helps stabilize attention, keeping us mindful and alert. Bringing the mind back to a primary object, like the breath, takes a certain quality of effort, and that effort builds energy. It is like doing a repetitive exercise to develop muscular strength. You keep doing it and the body gets stronger. Coming back to the primary object is mental exercise. We come back to the breath, again and again, and slowly the mind grows stronger and more stable. Our level of energy rises. Then when we open to a more choiceless awareness, we perceive things in a more refined and powerful way.

If at times you feel constriction or strain in the practice, it helps to settle back and open the field of awareness. Leave the breath for a while and simply notice, in turn, whatever arises at the six sense doors (the five physical senses and the mind): hearing, seeing, pressure, tingling, thinking. Or you can rest in an open, natural awareness, paying attention only to sounds appearing and disappearing. Widening the focus of attention in this way helps the mind come to balance and spaciousness.

You can also use the technique of mental noting to strengthen mindful awareness. The art of mental noting, as a tool of meditation, requires practice and experimentation. Labeling objects of experience as they arise supports mindfulness in many different ways.

Noting should be done very softly, like a whisper in the mind, but with enough precision and accuracy so that it connects directly with the object. For example, you might label each breath, silently saying *in, out* or *falling*. In addition, you may also note every other appearance that arises in meditation. When thoughts arise, note *thinking*. If physical sensations become predominant, note *pressure, vibration, tension, tingling,* or whatever it might be. If sounds or images come into the foreground, note *hearing* or *seeing*.

The note itself can be seen as another appearance in the mind, even as it functions to keep us undistracted. Labeling, like putting a frame around a picture, helps you recognize the object more clearly and gives greater focus and precision to your observation.

Mental noting supports mindfulness in another way, by showing us when awareness is reactive and when it is truly mindful. For example, we may be aware of pain in the body, but through a filter of aversion. Without the tool of noting, we often do not recognize the aversion, which may be a subtle overlay on the pain itself. The tone of voice of the mental note reveals a lot about our minds. You sit and note, *pain, pain,* but perhaps with a gritted-teeth tone to the note, the tone makes obvious the actual state of mind. Quite amazingly, simply changing the tone of the note can often change your mind state. Noting refines the quality of mindfulness, that very particular, nonreactive awareness.

Mental labeling also strengthens the effort-energy factor in the mind. Because noting does take a special effort, some people find it difficult to do in the beginning. But effort overcomes sloth and torpor; the very effort to softly note each arising object arouses energy, which keeps the practice developing and deepening.

The skillful use of mental noting keeps us energized, accurate, and mindful. Try this technique in your next sitting, even if only for a short period of time at first. Simply note each arising appearance as you become aware of it: *rising, falling, thinking, thinking; pain, pain; rising, falling.* Frame each moment of experience with a soft mental note, and observe the difference in the quality of your attention.

Be patient in learning to use this tool of practice. Sometimes people note too loudly, and it overshadows the experience. Sometimes people try too hard, becoming tight and tense with the effort. Let the note float down on the object, like a butterfly landing on a flower, or let it float up with the object, like a bubble rising. Be light, be soft, have fun.

# Kosho Uchiyama

## Open the Hand of Thought

*One of the most common experiences for new and old meditators alike—whether their tradition is Tibetan, Zen, or Vipassana—is having attention derailed by thoughts. Zen master Uchiyama contrasted thinking and meditation—people and rocks.*

[IF] YOU SIT and think during zazen, then that is thinking and not zazen. Does that mean no thoughts at all should occur to us during zazen? Is good zazen that condition when all thoughts have ceased to come into our minds?

Here we have to clearly distinguish "chasing after thoughts and thinking" from "ideas or thoughts occurring." If a thought occurs during zazen and we proceed to chase after it, then we are thinking and not doing zazen. Yet this doesn't mean that we are doing zazen only when thoughts have entirely ceased to occur. How should we understand this contradiction?

Imagine placing a large rock next to a person doing zazen. Since this rock is not alive, no matter how long it sits there, a thought will never occur to it. Unlike the rock, however, the person doing zazen next to it is a living human being.

Even if we sit as stationary as the rock, we cannot say that no thoughts will occur. On the contrary, if they did not, we would have to say that that person is no longer alive. But, of course, the truth of life never means to become lifeless like the rock. For that reason, thoughts ceasing to occur is not the ideal state of one sitting zazen. It is perfectly natural that thoughts occur. Yet, if we chase after thoughts, we are thinking and no longer doing zazen. So what should our attitude be?

Briefly, aiming at maintaining the posture of zazen with our flesh and bones, letting go of thoughts, is the most appropriate expression for describing what our attitude should be. What is letting go of thoughts? Well, when we think, we think of *something*. Thinking of something means grasping that something with thought. However, during zazen we open the hand of thought that is trying to grasp something, and simply refrain from grasping. This is letting go of thoughts.

# Jack Kornfield

## Sangha and Retreat

*The Buddha stressed that being part of a sangha, or community,
and periodic retreats were critically important for practice. Some
2,500 year later, Vipassana teacher Jack Kornfield reinforces
that observation.*

IN SUSTAINING A life of mindfulness, it is extremely
helpful to connect with other people who share the same
values and orientation. Once the disciple Ananda spoke to
the Buddha, saying, "It seems to me that half of the holy
life is association with good and noble friends."

The Buddha replied, "Not so, Ananda. The whole of the
holy life is association with good and noble friends, with
noble practices, and with noble ways of living."

The support and encouragement we give one another in
practice is extremely important and powerful. It's difficult
to practice alone, particularly in a culture such as ours,
which continually bombards us with messages saying, "Live
for the future." "Do this and get that and become this and
have that, and you will be happy." One of the blessings of
joining a traditional community of monks and nuns is the

sense of support such a sangha can give. As lay people we can find that support invaluable as well. Connecting with other people involved in spiritual practice renews our inspiration and energy. It can help keep practice alive for us in times when our motivation has waned. It can provide a way for us to support and inspire others, which itself is very strengthening to our practice.

Sit with others. If there is no sitting group meeting together regularly in your area, then start one and list it in [your practice's] newspapers. If there aren't other people doing [your practice], then sit with other Buddhist groups in your area, or sit at the local silent Quaker meetings. Joining together with anyone who understands the value of taking time to turn inward, to quiet the mind and develop awareness, is very, very helpful.

In the same way, taking periods of silence and retreat regularly throughout the year is important for the renewal and deepening of practice. Regular meditation retreats are an obvious support. So too are personal retreats alone at home or at a retreat center. Similarly days of retreat and rest in nature, hiking in the mountains or along the ocean, times of silence and listening are all nurturing to practice. It is not by accident that many of the world's greatest monasteries and spiritual centers are in forests and remote places of beauty. Silent time can renew our spirits and reconnect us with the simplicity of practice.

Just as we will discover opening and closing cycles of the heart, and up and down cycles in our meditation, there are also greater cycles of silence and service over the years of our practice. Sometimes all that we need is a quiet space in which to meditate and listen. Other cycles pull us to family life, world service, community relations—a mindful life in the world. When we work with developing a silent inner meditation, only some of what we cultivate in one area carries over to the other. Just as we must actively choose to develop consciousness in a very focused way in sitting or a panoramic way in walking, we must also choose to develop mindfulness in driving or in our relationships. In this way, we can build upon the strengths of our initial meditation practice developed in silent retreats. We can bring the power of mindfulness into all the areas of our life.

# POSTURE

*With this general background, let's look more closely at specific elements of meditation and kinds of practice, beginning with posture. These guidelines for posture generally adhere to those handed down over the centuries, but there are tips that seem especially relevant to today's practitioners from Theravadan teacher Venerable Henepola Gunaratana, Tibetan nun Kathleen McDonald, and Zen master Shunryo Suzuki.*

## Venerable Henepola Gunaratana

### What to Do with Your Body

THE PRACTICE OF meditation has been going on for several thousand years. That is quite a bit of time for experimentation, and the procedure has been very, very thoroughly refined. Buddhist practice has always recognized that the mind and body are tightly linked and that each influences the other. Thus, there are certain recommended physical practices which will greatly help you to master this skill. And these practices should be followed. Keep in mind, however, that these postures are practice aids. Don't confuse the two. Meditation does not mean sitting in the lotus position. It is a mental skill. It can be practiced anywhere you wish. But these postures will help you to learn this skill and they speed your progress and development. So use them.

## GENERAL RULES

The purpose of the various postures is threefold. First, they provide a stable feeling in the body. This allows you to remove your attention from such issues as balance and muscular fatigue, so that you can center your concentration on the formal object of meditation. Second, they promote physical immobility which is then reflected by an immobility of mind. This creates a deeply settled and tranquil concentration. Third, they give you the ability to sit for a long period of time without yielding to the meditator's three main enemies—pain, muscular tension, and falling asleep.

The most essential thing is to sit with your back straight. The spine should be erect with the spinal vertebrae held like a stack of coins, one on top of the other. Your head should be held in line with the rest of the spine. All of this is done in a relaxed manner. No stiffness. You are not a wooden soldier, and there is no drill sergeant. There should be no muscular tension involved in keeping the back straight. Sit light and easy. The spine should be like a firm young tree growing out of soft ground. The rest of the body just hangs from it in a loose, relaxed manner. This is going to require a bit of experimentation on your part. We generally sit in tight, guarded postures when we are walking or talking and in sprawling postures when we are relaxing. Neither of those will do. But they are cultural habits and they can be relearned.

Your objective is to achieve a posture in which you can sit for the entire session without moving at all. In the beginning you will probably feel a bit odd to sit with a straight back. But you will get used to it. It takes practice, and an erect posture is very important. This is what is known in physiology as a position of arousal, and with it goes mental alertness. If you slouch, you are inviting drowsiness. What you sit on is equally important. You are going to need a chair or a cushion, depending on the posture you choose, and the firmness of the seat must be chosen with some care. Too soft a seat can put you right to sleep. Too hard can promote pain.

## CLOTHING

The clothes you wear for meditation should be loose and soft. If they restrict blood flow or put pressure on nerves, the result will be pain and/or that tingling numbness which we normally refer to as our "legs going to sleep." If you are wearing a belt, loosen it. Don't wear tight pants or pants made of thick material. Long skirts are a good choice for women. Loose pants made of thin or elastic material are fine for anybody. Soft, flowing robes are the traditional garb in Asia and they come in an enormous variety of styles such as sarongs and kimonos. Take your shoes off, and if your stockings are tight and binding, take them off, too.

## TRADITIONAL POSTURES

When you are sitting on the floor in the traditional Asian manner, you need a cushion to elevate your spine. Choose one that is relatively firm and at least three inches thick when compressed. Sit close to the front edge of the cushion and let your crossed legs rest on the floor in front of you. If the floor is carpeted, that may be enough to protect your shins and ankles from pressure. If it is not, you will probably need some sort of padding for your legs. A folded blanket will do nicely. Don't sit all the way back on the cushion. This position causes its front edge to press into the underside of your thigh, causing nerves to pinch. The result will be leg pain.

There are a number of ways you can fold your legs. We'll list four in ascending order of preference.

a. *American Indian style.* Your right foot is tucked under the left knee and your left foot is tucked under your right knee.
b. *Burmese style.* Both of your legs lie flat on the floor from knee to foot. They are parallel with each other and one in front of the other.

c. *Half lotus*. Both of your knees touch the floor. One leg and foot lie flat along the calf of the other leg.

d. *Full lotus*. Both knees touch the floor, and your legs are crossed at the calf. Your left foot rests on the right thigh, and your right foot rests on the left thigh. Both soles turn upward.

In all these postures, your hands are cupped one on the other, and they rest on your lap with the palms turned upward. The hands lie just below the navel with the bend of each wrist pressed against the thigh. This arm position provides firm bracing for the upper body. Don't tighten your neck or shoulder muscles. Relax your arms. Your diaphragm is held relaxed, expanded to maximum fullness. Don't let tension build up in the stomach area. Your chin is up. Your eyes can be open or closed. If you keep them open, fix them on the tip of your nose or in a middle distance straight in front. You are not looking at anything. You are just putting your eyes where there is nothing in particular to see, so that you can forget about vision. Don't strain, don't stiffen, and don't be rigid. Relax; let the body be natural and supple. Let it hang from the erect spine like a rag doll.

Half and full lotus positions are the traditional meditation postures in Asia. And the full lotus is considered the best. It is the most solid by far. Once you are locked into this position, you can be completely immovable for a very long period. Since it requires a considerable flexibility in the legs, not everybody can do it. Besides, the main criterion by which you choose a posture for yourself is not what others say about it. It is your own comfort. Choose a position that allows you to sit the longest without pain, without moving. Experiment with different postures. The tendons will loosen with practice. And then you can work gradually toward the full lotus.

## USING A CHAIR

Sitting on the floor may not be feasible for you because of pain or some other reason. No problem. You can always use a chair instead. Pick one that has a level seat, a straight back and no arms. It is best to sit in such a way that your back does not lean against the back of the chair. The furniture of the seat should not dig into the underside of your thighs. Place your legs side by side, feet flat on the floor. As with the traditional postures, place both hands on your lap, cupped one upon the other. Don't tighten your neck or shoulder muscles, and relax your arms. Your eyes can be open or closed.

In all the above postures, remember your objectives. You want to achieve a state of complete physical stillness, yet you don't want to fall asleep. Recall the analogy of the muddy water. You want to promote a totally settled state of the body which will engender a corresponding mental settling. There must also be a state of physical alertness which can induce the kind of mental clarity you seek. So experiment. Your body is a tool for creating desired mental states. Use it judiciously.

# Kathleen McDonald

## *Seven-Point Posture*

MIND AND BODY are interdependent. Because the state of one affects the state of the other, a correct sitting posture is emphasized for meditation. The seven-point posture, used by experienced meditators for centuries, is recommended as the best way to help gain a calm, clear state of mind.

## 1. LEGS

If possible, sit with your legs crossed in the vajra, or full-lotus, position where each foot is placed, sole upward, on the thigh of the opposite leg. This position is difficult to maintain but by practicing each day you will find that your body slowly adapts and you are able to sit this way for increasingly longer periods. The vajra posture gives the best support to the body, but is not essential.

An alternative position is the half-lotus where the left foot is on the floor under the right leg and the right foot on top of the left thigh. You can also sit in a simple cross-legged posture with both feet on the floor.

A firm cushion under the buttocks will enable you to keep your back straight and sit longer without getting pins-and-needles in your legs and feet.

If you are unable to sit on the floor in any of these positions, you can meditate in a chair or on a low, slanted bench. The important thing is to be comfortable.


## 2. ARMS

Hold your hands loosely on your lap, about two inches below the navel, right hand on top of the left, palms upward, with the fingers aligned. The two hands should be slightly cupped so that the tips of the thumbs meet to form a triangle. Shoulders and arms should be relaxed. Your arms should not be pressed against your body but held a few inches away to allow circulation of air: this helps to prevent sleepiness.

## 3. BACK

Your back is most important. It should be straight, held relaxed and lightly upright, as if the vertebrae were a pile of coins. It might be difficult in the beginning, but in time it will become natural and you will notice the benefits: your energy will flow more freely, you won't feel sluggish and you will be able to sit comfortably in meditation for increasingly longer periods.

## 4. EYES

New meditators often find it easier to concentrate with their eyes fully closed. This is quite acceptable. However, it is recommended that you leave your eyes slightly open to admit a little light, and direct your gaze downwards. Closing your eyes may be an invitation to sluggishness, sleep or dream-like images, all of which hinder meditation.

## 5. JAW

Your jaw should be relaxed and teeth slightly apart, not clenched. Your mouth should also be relaxed, with the lips together lightly.

## 6. TONGUE

The tip of your tongue should touch the palate just behind the upper teeth. This reduces the flow of saliva and thus the need to swallow, both of which are hindrances as your concentration increases and you sit in meditation for longer periods.

## 7. HEAD

Your neck should be bent forward a little so that your gaze is directed naturally towards the floor in front of you. If your head is held too high you may have problems with mental wandering and agitation, and if dropped too low you could experience mental heaviness or sleepiness.

This seven-point posture is most conducive to clear, unobstructed contemplation. You might find it difficult in the beginning, but it is a good idea to go through each point at the start of your session and try to maintain the correct posture for a few minutes. With familiarity it will feel more natural and you will begin to notice its benefits.

The practice of hatha yoga or other physical disciplines can be a great help in loosening tight muscles and joints, thus enabling you to sit more comfortably. However, if you are unable to adapt to sitting cross-legged you can make a compromise between perfect posture and a relaxed state. In other words, keep your body and mind happy, comfortable and free of tension.

# Shunryu Suzuki

## The Oneness of Duality

NOW I WOULD like to talk about our zazen posture. When you sit in the full lotus position, your left foot is on your right thigh, and your right foot is on your left thigh. When we cross our legs like this, even though we have a right leg and a left leg, they have become one. The position expresses the oneness of duality: not two, and not one. This is the most important teaching: not two, and not one. Our body and mind are not two and not one. If you think your body and mind are two, that is wrong; if you think that they are one, that is also wrong. Our body and mind are both two *and* one. We usually think that if something is not one, it is more than one; if it is not singular, it is plural. But in actual experience, our life is not only plural, but also singular. Each one of us is both dependent and independent.

After some years we will die. If we just think that it is
the end of our life, this will be the wrong understanding.
But, on the other hand, if we think that we do not die, this
is also wrong. We die, and we do not die. This is the right
understanding. Some people may say that our mind or soul
exists forever, and it is only our physical body which dies.
But this is not exactly right, because both mind and body
have their end. But at the same time it is also true that they
exist eternally. And even though we say mind and body,
they are actually two sides of one coin. This is the right
understanding. So when we take this posture it symbolizes
this truth. When I have the left foot on the right side of
my body, and the right foot on the left side of my body, I
do not know which is which. So either may be the left or
the right side.

The most important thing in taking the zazen posture is
to keep your spine straight. Your ears and your shoulders
should be on one line. Relax your shoulders, and push up
towards the ceiling with the back of your head. And you
should pull your chin in. When your chin is tilted up, you
have no strength in your posture; you are probably dreaming. Also to gain strength in your posture, press your diaphragm down towards your *hara,* or lower abdomen. This
will help you maintain your physical and mental balance.
When you try to keep this posture, at first you may find
some difficulty breathing naturally, but when you get ac-
customed to it you will be able to breathe naturally and
deeply.

Your hands should form the "cosmic mudra." If you put your left hand on top of your right, middle joints of your middle fingers together, and touch your thumbs lightly together (as if you held a piece of paper between them), your hands will make a beautiful oval. You should keep this universal mudra with great care, as if you were holding something very precious in your hand. Your hands should be held against your body, with your thumbs at about the height of your navel. Hold your arms freely and easily, and slightly away from your body, as if you held an egg under each arm without breaking it.

You should not be tilted sideways, backwards, or forwards. You should be sitting straight up as if you were supporting the sky with your head. This is not just form or breathing. It expresses the key point of Buddhism. It is a perfect expression of your Buddha nature. If you want true understanding of Buddhism, you should practice this way. These forms are not a means of obtaining the right state of mind. To take this posture itself is the purpose of our practice. When you have this posture, you have the right state of mind, so there is no need to try to attain some special state. . . .

So try always to keep the right posture, not only when you practice zazen, but in all your activities. Take the right posture when you are driving your car, and when you are reading. If you read in a slumped position, you cannot stay awake long. Try. You will discover how important it is to keep the right posture. This is the true teaching. The teaching which is written on paper is not the true teaching. Written teaching is a kind of food for your brain. Of course it is necessary to take some food for your brain, but it is more important to be yourself by practicing the right way of life.

That is why Buddha could not accept the religions existing at his time. He studied many religions, but he was not satisfied with their practices. He could not find the answer in asceticism or in philosophies. He was not interested in some metaphysical existence, but in his own body and mind, here and now. And when he found himself, he found that everything that exists has Buddha nature. That was his enlightenment. Enlightenment is not some good feeling or some particular state of mind. The state of mind that exists when you sit in the right posture is, itself, enlightenment. If you cannot be satisfied with the state of mind you have in zazen, it means your mind is still wandering about. Our body and mind should not be wobbling or wandering about. In this posture there is no need to talk about the right state of mind. You already have it. This is the conclusion of Buddhism.

# Jon Kabat-Zinn

## *Dignity*

*When we sit in a formal posture, there is a subtle internal experience that goes beyond strict alignment. Jon Kabat-Zinn expresses it as dignity.*

WHEN WE DESCRIBE the sitting posture, the word that feels the most appropriate is "dignity."

Sitting down to meditate, our posture talks to us. It makes its own statement. You might say the posture itself is the meditation. If we slump, it reflects low energy, passivity, a lack of clarity. If we sit ramrod-straight, we are tense, making too much of an effort, trying too hard. When I use the word "dignity" in teaching situations, as in "Sit in a way that embodies dignity," everybody immediately adjusts their posture to sit up straighter. But they don't stiffen. Faces relax, shoulders drop, head, neck, and back come into easy alignment. The spine rises out of the pelvis with energy. Sometimes people tend to sit forward, away from the backs of their chairs, more autonomously.

Everybody seems to instantly know that inner feeling of dignity and how to embody it. . . .

So, when we take our seat in meditation and remind ourselves to sit with dignity, we are coming back to our original worthiness. . . .

# BREATHING

*Sitting in dignity, we bring our awareness to the object of our awareness. The Buddha's* Anapanasati Sutta, *or* Sutra on the Full Awareness of Breathing, *established the breath as that object. In this translation by Vietnamese Zen teacher Thich Nhat Hanh, the Buddha lays out unequivocally how meditation on the breath is the basis of all of Buddhist practice. Seventeenth-century Zen master Man-an describes how following this practice can produce great joyfulness.*

## The Buddha

### *Sutra on the Full Awareness of Breathing*

"OBHIKKHUS, THE METHOD of being fully aware of breathing, if developed and practiced continuously, will have great rewards and bring great advantages. It will lead to success in practicing the Four Establishments of Mindfulness. If the method of the Four Establishments of Mindfulness is developed and practiced continuously, it will lead to success in the practice of the Seven Factors of Awakening. The Seven Factors of Awakening, if developed and practiced continuously, will give rise to Understanding and Liberation of the Mind.

"What is the way to develop and practice continuously

the method of Full Awareness of Breathing so that the practice will be rewarding and offer great benefit?

"It is like this, bhikkhus: the practitioner goes into the forest or to the foot of a tree, or to any deserted place, and sits stably in the lotus position, holding his body quite straight. Breathing in, he knows that he is breathing in; and breathing out, he knows that he is breathing out.

1. Breathing in a long breath, he knows, 'I am breathing in a long breath.' Breathing out a long breath, he knows, 'I am breathing out a long breath.'
2. Breathing in a short breath, he knows, 'I am breathing in a short breath.' Breathing out a short breath, he knows, 'I am breathing out a short breath.'
3. 'I am breathing in and am aware of my whole body. I am breathing out and am aware of my whole body.' This is how he practices.
4. 'I am breathing in and making my whole body calm and at peace. I am breathing out and making my whole body calm and at peace.' This is how he practices.
5. 'I am breathing in and feeling joyful. I am breathing out and feeling joyful.' This is how he practices.
6. 'I am breathing in and feeling happy. I am breathing out and feeling happy.' He practices like this.
7. 'I am breathing in and am aware of the activities of the mind in me. I am breathing out and am aware of the activities of the mind in me.' He practices like this.
8. 'I am breathing in and making the activities of the mind in me calm and at peace. I am breathing out and making

the activities of the mind in me calm and at peace.' He practices like this.

9. 'I am breathing in and am aware of my mind. I am breathing out and am aware of my mind.' He practices like this.

10. 'I am breathing in and making my mind happy and at peace. I am breathing out and making my mind happy and at peace.' He practices like this.

11. 'I am breathing in and concentrating my mind. I am breathing out and concentrating my mind.' He practices like this.

12. 'I am breathing in and liberating my mind. I am breathing out and liberating my mind.' He practices like this.

13. 'I am breathing in and observing the impermanent nature of all dharmas. I am breathing out and observing the impermanent nature of all dharmas.' He practices like this.

14. 'I am breathing in and observing the fading of all dharmas. I am breathing out and observing the fading of all dharmas.' He practices like this.

15. 'I am breathing in and observing liberation. I am breathing out and observing liberation.' He practices like this.

16. 'I am breathing in and observing letting go. I am breathing out and observing letting go.' He practices like this.

"The Full Awareness of Breathing, if developed and practiced continuously according to these instructions, will be rewarding and of great benefit."

"In what way does one develop and continuously practice the Full Awareness of Breathing, in order to succeed in the practice of the Four Establishments of Mindfulness?

"When the practitioner breathes in or breathes out a long or a short breath, aware of his breath or his whole body, or aware that he is making his whole body calm and at peace, he abides peacefully in the observation of the body in the body, persevering, fully awake, clearly understanding his state, gone beyond all attachment and aversion to this life. In this case, breathing in and breathing out with Full Awareness belong to the first Establishment of Mindfulness, namely the body.

"When the practitioner breathes in or out with the awareness of joy or happiness, or awareness of the activities of the mind; when the practitioner breathes in or out in order to make the activities of his mind calm and at peace, at that time he abides peacefully in the observation of the feelings in the feelings, persevering, fully awake, clearly understanding his state, gone beyond all attachment and aversion to this life. This exercise of breathing with awareness belongs to the second Establishment of Mindfulness, namely the feelings.

"When the practitioner breathes in or breathes out with the awareness of the mind, or to make the mind calm and at peace, to collect the mind in concentration, or to free and liberate the mind, at that time he abides peacefully in the observation of the mind in the mind, persevering, fully awake, clearly understanding his state, gone beyond all attachment and aversion to this life. Without full awareness of breathing, there can be no development of meditative stability and understanding.

"When the practitioner breathes in or breathes out and contemplates the essential impermanence or the essential fading of all dharmas or liberation or letting go, at that time he abides peacefully in the awareness of the objects of the mind, persevering, fully awake, clearly understanding his state, gone beyond all attachment and aversion to this life.

"The practice of Full Awareness of Breathing, if developed and practiced continuously, will lead to perfect accomplishment of the Four Establishments of Mindfulness.

"Moreover, if they are developed and continuously practiced, the Four Establishments of Mindfulness will lead to perfect abiding in the Seven Factors of Awakening. How is this so?

"When the practitioner can maintain, without distraction, the practice of observing the body in the body, the feelings in the feelings, the mind in the mind, and the objects of mind in the objects of mind, persevering, fully awake, clearly understanding his state, gone beyond all attachment and aversion to this life, with unwavering, steadfast, imperturbable meditative stability, he will attain the first Factor of Awakening, namely full attention. When this factor is developed, it will come to perfection.

"When the practitioner can abide in meditative stability without being distracted and can investigate every dharma, every object of mind that arises, then the second Factor of Awakening will be born and developed in him, the factor of investigating dharmas. When this factor is developed, it will come to perfection.

"When the practitioner can observe and investigate every dharma in a sustained, persevering, and steadfast way, without being distracted, the third Factor of Awakening will be born and developed in him, the factor of energy. When this factor is developed, it will come to perfection.

"When the practitioner has reached a stable, imperturbable abiding in the stream of practice, the fourth Factor of Awakening will be born and developed in him, the factor of joy. When this factor is developed, it will come to perfection.

"When the practitioner can abide undistractedly in the state of joy, he will feel his body and mind light and at peace. At this point the fifth Factor of Awakening will be born and developed, the factor of ease. When this factor is developed, it will come to perfection.

"When both body and mind are at ease, the practitioner can easily enter into concentration. At that time the sixth Factor of Awakening will be born and developed in him, the factor of concentration. When this factor is developed, it will come to perfection.

"When the practitioner is abiding in concentration with deep calmness, he will cease discriminating and comparing. At that time the seventh factor of Awakening is released, born, and developed in him, the factor of letting go. When this factor is developed, it will come to perfection.

"This is how the Four Establishments of Mindfulness, if developed and practiced continuously, will lead to perfect abiding in the Seven Factors of Awakening.

"How will the Seven Factors of Awakening, if developed and practiced continuously, lead to the perfect accomplishment of true understanding and complete liberation?

"If the practitioner follows the path of the Seven Factors of Awakening, living in quiet seclusion, observing and contemplating the fading of all dharmas, he will develop the capacity of letting go. This will be a result of following the path of the Seven Factors of Awakening and will lead to the perfect accomplishment of true understanding and complete liberation."

# Zen Master Man-an

## *Tuning the Breathing*

A S  F O R  T H E  method of tuning the breathing, after having settled in your seat, nurture your mental energy in the ocean of energy and field of elixir, not letting it push upward from the umbilical sphere. Breathe through the nose, neither too rapidly nor too slowly, neither panting nor puffing.

When you breathe out, know you are breathing out; when you breathe in, know you are breathing in. Focus your consciousness on your breathing, not letting consciousness go up or down or out or in, not thinking discursively, not making intellectual or emotional interpretations, not trying to figure anything out, simply being aware of outgoing and incoming breathing, not missing a single breath.

When this concentration becomes continuous, the physical elements of the body become well tuned, the internal organs are purified, the upper parts are clear and cool, while the lower parts are warm. Body and mind will spontaneously produce great joyfulness.

# Venerable Henepola Gunaratana

## Taming a Wild Elephant

*The Venerable Henepola Gunaratana notes that before the joy produced in focused breathing arrives, training the mind is much like training a wild elephant, then explains why the breath has been chosen and used as this focus.*

WE USE BREATH as our focus. It serves as that vital reference point from which the mind wanders and is drawn back. Distraction cannot be seen as distraction unless there is some central focus to be distracted from. That is the frame of reference against which we can view the incessant changes and interruptions that go on all the time as a part of normal thinking.

Ancient Pali texts liken meditation to the process of taming a wild elephant. The procedure in those days was to tie a newly captured animal to a post with a good strong rope. When you do this, the elephant is not happy. He screams and tramples, and pulls against the rope for days. Finally it sinks through his skull that he can't get away, and he settles down. At this point you can begin to feed him and to handle him with some measure of safety. Eventually you can dispense with the rope and post altogether, and train your elephant for various tasks. Now you've got a tamed elephant that can be put to useful work. In this analogy the wild elephant is your wildly active mind, the rope is mindfulness, and the post is our object of meditation, our breathing. The tamed elephant who emerges from this process is a well-trained, concentrated mind that can then be used for the exceedingly tough job of piercing the layers of illusion that obscure reality. Meditation tames the mind.

The next question we need to address is: Why choose breathing as the primary object of meditation? Why not something a bit more interesting? Answers to this are numerous. A useful object of meditation should be one that promotes mindfulness. It should be portable, easily available and cheap. It should also be something that will not embroil us in those states of mind from which we are trying to free ourselves, such as greed, anger, and delusion. Breathing satisfies all these criteria and more. Breathing is something common to every human being. We all carry it with us wherever we go. It is always there, constantly available, never ceasing from birth till death, and it costs nothing.

Breathing is a non-conceptual process, a thing that can be experienced directly without a need for thought. Furthermore, it is a very living process, an aspect of life that is in constant change. The breath moves in cycles—inhalation, exhalation, breathing in, and breathing out. Thus, it is a miniature model of life itself.

The sensation of breath is subtle, yet it is quite distinct

when you learn to tune into it. It takes a bit of an effort to find it. Yet anybody can do it. You've got to work at it, but not too hard. For all these reasons, breathing makes an ideal object of meditation. Breathing is normally an involuntary process, proceeding at its own pace without a conscious will. Yet a single act of will can slow it down or speed it up, make it long and smooth or short and choppy. The balance between involuntary breathing and forced manipulation of breath is quite delicate. And there are lessons to be learned here on the nature of will and desire. Then, too, that point at the tip of the nostril can be viewed as a sort of a window between the inner and outer worlds. It is a nexus point and energy-transfer spot where stuff from the outside world moves in and becomes a part of what we call ''me,'' and where a part of ''me'' flows forth to merge with the outside world. There are lessons to be learned here about self-concept and how we form it.

Breath is a phenomenon common to all living things. A true experiential understanding of the process moves you closer to other living beings. It shows you your inherent connectedness with all of life. Finally, breathing is a present-time process. By that we mean it is always occurring in the here-and-now. We don't normally live in the present, of course. We spend most of our time caught up in memories of the past or looking ahead to the future, full of worries and plans. The breath has none of that ''other-timeness.'' When we truly observe the breath, we are automatically placed in the present. We are pulled out of the morass of mental images and into a bare experience of the here-and-now. In this sense, breath is a living slice of reality. A mindful observation of such a miniature model of life itself leads to insights that are broadly applicable to the rest of our experience.

The first step in using the breath as an object of meditation is to find it. What you are looking for is the physical sensation of the air that passes in and out of the nostrils. This is usually just inside the tip of the nose. But the exact spot varies from one person to another, depending on the shape of the nose. To find your own point, take a quick deep breath and notice the point just inside the nose or on the upper lip where you have the most distinct sensation of passing air. Now exhale and notice the sensation at the same point. It is from this point that you will follow the whole passage of breath. Once you have located your own breath point with clarity, don't deviate from that spot. Use this single point in order to keep your attention fixed. Without having selected such a point, you will find yourself moving in and out of the nose, going up and down the windpipe, eternally chasing after the breath which you can never catch because it keeps changing, moving, and flowing.

If you ever sawed wood you already know the trick. As a carpenter, you don't stand there watching the saw blade going up and down. You would get dizzy. You fix your attention on the spot where the teeth of the blade dig into the wood. It is the only way you can saw a straight line. As a meditator, you focus your attention on that single spot of sensation inside the nose. From this vantage point, you watch the entire movement of breath with clear and collected attention. Make no attempt to control the breath. This is not a breathing exercise of the sort done in Yoga. Focus on the natural and spontaneous movement of the breath. Don't try to regulate it or emphasize it in any way. Most beginners have some trouble in this area. In order to help themselves focus on the sensation, they unconsciously accentuate their breathing. The result is a forced and unnatural effort that actually inhibits concentration rather than helping it. Don't increase the depth of your breath or its sound. This latter point is especially important in group meditation. Loud breathing can be a real annoyance to those around you. Just let the breath move naturally, as if you were asleep. Let go and allow the process to go along at its own rhythm.

This sounds easy, but it is trickier than you think. Do not be discouraged if you find your own will getting in the way. Just use that as an opportunity to observe the nature of conscious intention. Watch the delicate interrelation between the breath, the impulse to control the breath, and the impulse to cease controlling the breath. You may find it frustrating for a while, but it is highly profitable as a learning experience, and it is a passing phase. Eventually, the breathing process will move along under its own steam, and you will feel no impulse to manipulate it. At this point you will have learned a major lesson about your own compulsive need to control the universe.

# Shunryu Suzuki

## The Swinging Door

*When the wild elephant has been tamed, our breath is like a door,*
*Zen master Shunryu Suzuki notes, swinging between the inner world*
*and the outer world.*

WHEN WE PRACTICE zazen our mind always follows our breathing. When we inhale, the air comes into the inner world. When we exhale, the air goes out to the outer world. The inner world is limitless, and the outer world is also limitless. We say "inner world" or "outer world," but actually there is just one whole world. In this limitless world, our throat is like a swinging door. The air comes in and goes out like someone passing through a swinging door. If you think, "I breathe," the "I" is extra. There is no you to say "I." What we call "I" is just a swinging door which moves when we inhale and when we exhale. It just moves; that is all. When your mind is pure and calm enough to follow this movement, there is nothing: no "I," no world, no mind nor body; just a swinging door.

So when we practice zazen, all that exists is the movement of the breathing, but we are aware of this movement. You should not be absentminded. But to be aware of the movement does not mean to be aware of your small self, but rather of your universal nature, or Buddha nature. This kind of awareness is very important, because we are usually so one-sided. Our usual understanding of life is dualistic: you and I, this and that, good and bad. But actually these discriminations are themselves the awareness of the universal existence. "You" means to be aware of the universe in the form of you, and "I" means to be aware of it in the form of I. You and I are just swinging doors. This kind of understanding is necessary. This should not even be called understanding; it is actually the true experience of life through Zen practice.

# Ayya Khema

## Ways of Using the Breath

*Just as full awareness of breathing is the experience of life itself, so too, observes Theravadan nun Ayya Khema, can the practice in formal meditation support our mindfulness in everyday life.*

WHEN WE LISTEN to the words of the Buddha, we know that he is showing us an ideal to work for, and that if we have not yet reached that ideal we need not blame ourselves. "Awareness, no blame, change" is an important formula to remember: to become aware of what is going on within oneself but not to attach any blame to it. Things are the way they are, but we, as thinking human beings, have the ability to change and that is what we are doing in meditation. . . .

If we can learn to use mindfulness of the breath in meditation, then we have a very good grip on mindfulness in everyday life. Each supports the other. It is impossible to make two people out of each one of us; we are training only one mind. Obviously the time spent on our daily activities far exceeds the time we spend in meditation.

Therefore we cannot just drop all training when we step out of the meditation room.

There are five ways of using the breath. The most traditional, which is the most difficult but also the most productive of calm, is to watch the breath at the nostrils as it moves in and out. In our tradition we watch both in- and out-breaths; we do not wish to give the mind a chance to wander off into its usual discursiveness, but want it to stay with the breath at all times. The breath is wind and creates a sensation when it touches the nostrils, which helps one to focus at that point. This is the most one-pointed way of concentrating on the breath, but also the most demanding, and it is particularly useful for experienced meditators. ("One-pointedness" means being in one spot only, which is a very important aspect of meditation.) Because the attention is focused on one point only, it helps the mind to become sharp and unwavering.

We can use various support systems. One of these is counting the breaths. We count "one" on the in-breath, "one" on the out-breath, "two" on the in-breath, "two" on the out-breath, no further than ten. Every time the mind wanders off we return to "one." It's no use trying to figure out whether we were at four, five or eight or at least at nine, but we simply go back to "one." This is a good method for people who like numbers and who have orderly, organized minds. . . .

If the mind wants to run off, it is useful to direct the attention towards the impermanence of the breath. The untrained mind always wants to think, but at least we can give it something useful to think about. It doesn't have to be allowed to think about whatever it pleases, but rather how each in-breath finishes, then each out-breath likewise—constant change, on which our life depends. We could not stay alive without our breath coming and going all the time. If we were to keep the in-breath, we would be dead within a few minutes; the same would occur if we were to hang on to the out-breath. This is an important insight which can link the mind to the impermanent aspect of each person, particularly ourselves. . . .

Experiencing the impermanence of the breath brings useful insight and is immensely preferable to thoughts about past or future. Being able to stay with the breath means that we are mindfully "in the moment." Absurd as it may seem, without training we hardly ever manage to do this. We can only live life each moment, and yet we are concerned with the past, which has gone irrevocably, and with the future, which is nothing but a hope and a prayer. When the future really comes, it is always called the present. We can never experience the future; it is nothing but a concept. If we want to gain wisdom, we have to experience life, and the only way we will ever do so is to be in each moment. The more we train the mind to be in each moment, the more we will actually know what human life means.

# Mahasi Sayadaw

## *Exercise / Breathing*

*Burmese Theravadan teacher Mahasi Sayadaw finds that especially for beginning meditators, focusing awareness on the abdomen is a helpful way to begin to focus on the breath.*

To BEGIN TRAINING, take the sitting posture, sit erect with legs crossed. You might feel more comfortable if the legs are not interlocked but evenly placed on the ground, without pressing one against the other. . . .

Try to keep your mind (but not your eyes) on the abdomen. You will thereby come to know the movements of rising and falling, the expansion and contraction of this organ. If these movements are not clear to you in the beginning, then place both hands on the abdomen to feel these rising and falling movements. After a short time the outward movement of inhalation and the inward movement of exhalation will become clear. Then make a mental note, *rising* for the outward movement, *falling* for the inward movement. Your mental note of each movement must be made while it occurs. From this exercise you learn the actual manner of the movements of the abdomen. You are not concerned with the form of the abdomen. What you actually perceive is the bodily sensation of pressure caused by the heaving movement of the abdomen. So do not dwell on the form of the abdomen but proceed with the exercise.

For the beginner it is a very effective method of developing the facilities of attention, concentration of mind and insight in contemplation. As practice increases, the manner of movement will be clearer. The ability to know each successive occurrence of the mental and physical processes at each of the six sense-organs is acquired only when insight contemplation is fully developed. Since you are a beginner whose attentiveness and power of concentration are still weak, you may find it difficult to keep the mind on each successive rising movement and falling movement as it occurs. In view of this difficulty, you may be inclined to think: "I just don't know how to keep my mind on each of these movements." Then simply remember that this is a learning process. The rising and falling movements of the abdomen are always present, and therefore there is no need to look for them. Actually with practice it becomes easy for a beginner to keep his mind on these two simple movements. Continue with this exercise in full awareness of the abdomen's rising and falling movements. Never verbally repeat the words *rising, falling,* although you may make a mental note *rising* and *falling* in the mind silently as they occur. Be clearly aware only of the actual process of the rising and falling movement of the abdomen. Avoid deep or rapid breathing for the purpose of making the abdominal movements more distinct, because this procedure causes fatigue that interferes with the practice. Just be totally aware of the movements of rising and falling as they occur in the course of normal breathing.

# WALKING

*The Buddha clearly identified breathing as the ideal focus for awareness, but in the* Mahasatipatthana Sutta: The Greater Discourse on the Foundations of Mindfulness, *he described the four foundations of mindfulness as awareness of the body as body, the mind as mind, the feelings as feelings, and mind-objects as mind-objects. We have begun, as he did, with breathing. Let us now broaden our possible objects of awareness of the body as body to walking.*

## The Buddha

## The Greater Discourse on the Foundations of Mindfulness

"Again, a monk, when walking, knows that he is walking, when standing, knows that he is standing, when sitting, knows that he is sitting, when lying down, knows that he is lying down. In whatever way his body is disposed, he knows that that is how it is. . . .

"Again, a monk, when going forward or back, is clearly aware of what he is doing, in looking forward or back he is clearly aware of what he is doing, in bending and stretching he is clearly aware of what he is doing, in carrying his inner and outer robe and his bowl he is clearly aware of what he is doing, in eating, drinking, chewing and savouring he is clearly aware of what he is doing . . .

"So he abides contemplating body as body internally, externally, and both internally and externally . . . And he abides independent, not clinging to anything in the world. And that, monks, is how a monk abides contemplating body as body."

# Hakuin Yasutani Roshi

## Kinhin

*We begin with Japanese Zen teacher Hakuin Yasutani Roshi, who suggests moving from sitting meditation into* kinhin, *a walking form of zazen.*

IN TERMINATING A period of sitting do not rise abruptly, but begin by rocking from side to side, first in small swings, then in large ones, for about half a dozen times. You will observe that your movements in this exercise are the reverse of those you engage in when you begin zazen. Rise slowly and quietly walk around with the others in what is called *kinhin,* a walking form of zazen.

Kinhin is performed by placing the right fist, with thumb inside, on the chest and covering it with the left palm while holding both palms at right angles. Keep the arms in a straight line and the body erect, with the eyes resting on a point about two yards in front of the feet. At the same time continue to count inhalations and exhalations as you walk slowly around the room. Begin walking with the left foot and walk in such a way that the foot sinks into the floor, first the heel and then the toes. Walk calmly and steadily, with poise and dignity. The walking must not be done absentmindedly, and the mind must be taut as you concentrate on the counting. It is advisable to practice walking this way for at least five minutes after each sitting period of twenty to thirty minutes.

You are to think of this walking as zazen in motion. Rinzai and Soto [the two main schools of Japanese Zen] differ considerably in their way of doing kinhin. In the Rinzai method the walking is brisk and energetic, while in the traditional Soto it is slow and leisurely; in fact, upon each breath you step forward only six inches or so. . . . Now, even though this walking relieves the stiffness in your legs, such exercise is to be regarded as a mere byproduct and not the main object of kinhin. Hence those of you who are counting your breaths should continue during kinhin, and those of you who are working on a koan should carry on with it.

# Joan Halifax

## *The Mind of Practice Embodied*

*Zen Buddhist teacher and ecologist Joan Halifax sees walking
meditation as the embodiment of our mind of practice.*

IN BUDDHISM WE practice aimlessness (*apranahita*),
even in relation to our personal, social, and environmen-
tal work. It means that we are not so purposive that we
destroy the present moment. "What way from here?" poet
Han Shan asks his shadow. Just this step. The path is every
step. How can we stray from it?

One day when I was walking down the canyon path in
Ojai [California], I realized that I was making a literal impression on the Earth. I stopped and turned around to look
at my footprints and they were even and smooth, a kind of
script in the dust. That was on Thursday. On Friday, I
hurried to the office on the central part of the land and
halfway there I caught myself, stopped and turned around
to look at my tracks. There was a different message on the
Earth. It was then that I saw how completely each step that

we take is a message of alienation or awareness to Earth. And it is in the experience of walking that we can learn this truth.

In Zen Buddhist practice, walking in the zendo is a way for us to stitch together our awareness with the world. One Zen master compared walking to the fine sewing of a robe, each step perfect and complete, each step resolved. I like to dwell on this image of the robe because it brings up the sense of precision and harmony that mindfulness cultivates.

Many years ago, I hurried along a trail in a cedar forest on one of the San Juan Islands near Seattle to see whether it was appropriate for a meditation walk. Hours later when I made the walk with twenty others, the world that had disappeared as I hurried through it in the morning was fully present as we walked in slow and quiet steps.

When we walk slowly, the world can fully appear. Not only are the creatures not frightened away by our haste or aggression, but the fine detail of fern and flower, or devastation and disruption, becomes visible. Many of us hurry along because we do not want to see what is really going on in and around us. We are afraid to let our senses touch the body of suffering or the body of beauty.

Walking meditation, for the Buddhist, is a way for the mind of practice to be embodied. Sitting in silence, stopping the body, makes it possible for the breath, mind, and body to calm down and finally synchronize. This is the practice of meditative stabilization, of balance, of the middle way of nonduality and nonviolence. . . . But walking meditation teaches us to move along without losing our mind and losing our balance. It teaches us how to ground our awareness with each step that we take. Walking practice is a kind of medicine that heals the split we experience from the world.

# Sylvia Boorstein

## *Exercise / Walking*

*Vipassana teacher Sylvia Boorstein now leads us step by step in walking meditation.*

PICK A PLACE to walk back and forth that is private and uncomplicated—one where the walking path can be ten to twenty feet long. If you walk outdoors, find a secluded spot so that you won't feel self-conscious. If you walk indoors, find a furniture-free section of your room or an empty hallway. Then you can devote all your attention to the feelings in your feet as you walk.

Keep in mind that this is attentiveness practice and tranquillity practice, not specialty walking practice. You don't need to walk in any unusual way. No special balance is needed, no special gracefulness. This is just plain walking. Perhaps at a slower pace than normal, but otherwise, quite ordinary.

Begin your period of practice by standing still for

a few moments at one end of your walking path. Close your eyes. Feel your whole body standing. Some people start by focusing their attention on the top of the head, then move their attention along the body through the head, shoulders, arms, torso, and legs, and end by feeling the sensations of the feet connecting with the earth. Allow your attention to rest on the sensations in the soles of the feet. This is likely to be the feeling of pressure on the feet and perhaps a sense of "soft" or "hard," depending on where you are standing.

Begin to walk forward. Keep your eyes open so that you stay balanced. I often begin with a normal strolling pace and expect that the limited scope of the walk, and its repetitious regularity, will naturally ease my body into a slower pace. Slowing down happens all by itself. I think it happens because the mind, with less stimuli to process, shifts into a lower gear. Probably the greed impulse, ever on the lookout for something novel to play with, surrenders when it realizes you're serious about not going anywhere.

When you walk at a strolling pace, the view is panoramic and descriptive. When your walking slows, the view is more localized and subjective. If we could see running readouts, like subtitles, of the mental notes that accompany walking, they might look like this:

*Strolling pace:* "Step . . . step . . . step . . . step

. . . arms moving . . . head moving . . . smiling . . . looking . . . stopping . . . turning . . . bird chirping . . . stepping . . . stepping . . . wondering what time it is . . . thinking this is boring . . . stepping . . . stepping . . . swinging arms . . . feeling warm . . . feeling cool . . . I'm glad I'm in the shade . . . deciding to stay in the shade . . . smiling . . . stepping . . .''

*Slower pace:* "Pressure on feet . . . pressure . . . pressure disappearing . . . pressure . . . reappearing . . . pressure . . . shifting . . . lightness . . . heaviness . . . lightness . . . heaviness . . . lightness . . . Hey! Now I've got it! Now I'm finally *present*! . . . Whoops, I've been distracted . . . Start again . . . Pressure on feet . . . pressure . . . shifting . . . lightness . . . heaviness . . . lightness . . . heaviness . . . hearing . . . warm . . . cool . . .''

Slow is not better than fast. It's just different. Everything changes, regardless of pace, and direct first-hand experience of temporality can happen while you are strolling just as much as while you are stepping deliberately and slowly. The speed-limit guide for mindful walking is to select the speed at which you are most likely to maintain attention. Shift up or down as necessary.

Now, try a period of walking meditation. Start with thirty minutes. If you have a timer with a pleasant "ding," set the timer and begin. If your watch has an alarm, you can use it as a timer. As you walk note how many times the impulse to check the time arises. Don't do it. Just walk. This way, in addition to composure and attentiveness, you get to practice renunciation, a fundamental factor in awakening.

# DRIVING

*When we do walking meditation, the point is not to get somewhere,
but rather to practice, using walking as the object of our attention.
Even when we do have to get somewhere and must drive to do so,
there is an opportunity for practice. Thich Nhat Hanh, Vietnamese
Zen master and poet, has written a number of gathas, or brief
verses, for enhancing our mindfulness during everyday activities,
even driving a car.*

# Thich Nhat Hanh

## Driving Meditation

*Before starting the car,
I know where I am going.
The car and I are one.
If the car goes fast, I go fast.*

IF WE ARE mindful when we start our car, we will know
how to use it properly. When we are driving, we tend
to think of arriving, and we sacrifice the journey for the
sake of the arrival. But life is to be found in the present
moment, not in the future. In fact, we may suffer more
after we arrive at our destination. If we have to talk of a

destination, what about our final destination, the graveyard? We do not want to go in the direction of death; we want to go in the direction of life. But where is life? Life can be found only in the present moment. Therefore, each mile we drive, each step we take, has to bring us into the present moment. This is the practice of mindfulness.

When we see a red light or a stop sign, we can smile at it and thank it, because it is a bodhisattva helping us return to the present moment. The red light is a bell of mindfulness. We may have thought of it as an enemy, preventing us from achieving our goal. But now we know the red light is our friend, helping us resist rushing and calling us to return to the present moment where we can meet with life, joy, and peace. Even if you are not the driver, you can help everyone in the car if you breathe and smile.

A number of years ago, I went to Canada to lead a retreat, and a friend took me across the city of Montreal. I noticed that every time a car stopped in front of me, I saw the sentence, *"Je me souviens"* ("I remember"), on the license plate. I did not know what they wanted to remember, perhaps their French-speaking origin, but it gave me an idea. I told my friend, "I have a present for all of you here. Every time you see a car stop in front of you with the line *'Je me souviens,'* you can see it as a bell of mindfulness helping you remember to breathe and smile. And you will have plenty of opportunities to breathe and smile while driving in Montreal."

My friend was delighted! He liked it so much that he

shared the practice with more than 200 people in the retreat. Later, when he came to visit me in France, he told me that Paris was not a good place to practice driving, as there were no signs *"Je me souviens."* I told him that he could practice with red lights and stop signs. After he left Plum Village and went back to Montreal, he wrote me a beautiful letter: "Thay, practicing in Paris was very easy. Not only did I practice with red lights and stop signs, but every time a car stopped in front of me, I saw the eyes of the Buddha blinking at me. I had to smile at those blinking eyes."

The next time you are caught in traffic, don't fight. It is useless to fight. If you sit back and smile to yourself, you will enjoy the present moment and make everyone in the car happy. The Buddha is there, because the Buddha can always be found in the present moment. Practicing meditation is to return to the present moment in order to encounter the flower, the blue sky, the child, the brilliant red light.

# EATING

*The Buddha's first teaching was given to a group of children from a small village near the tree of his enlightenment. As Thich Nhat Hanh describes, the Buddha made his teachings accessible to them through the experience of eating a tangerine.*

## Thich Nhat Hanh

### *Eating a Tangerine*

SIDDHARTHA [THE BUDDHA] quietly gestured for the children to sit back up and he said, "You are all intelligent children and I am sure you will be able to understand and practice the things I will share with you. The Great Path I have discovered is deep and subtle, but anyone willing to apply his or her heart and mind can understand and follow it.

"When you children peel a tangerine, you can eat it with awareness or without awareness. What does it mean to eat a tangerine in awareness? When you are eating the tangerine, you are aware that you are eating the tangerine. You fully experience its lovely fragrance and sweet taste. When you peel the tangerine, you know that you are peeling the tangerine; when you remove a slice and put it in your mouth, you know that you are removing a slice and putting it in your mouth; when you experience the lovely fragrance and sweet taste of the tangerine, you are aware that you are experiencing the lovely fragrance and sweet taste of the tangerine. The tangerine Nandabala offered me had nine sections. I ate each morsel in awareness and saw how precious and wonderful it was. I did not forget the tangerine, and thus the tangerine became something very real to me. If the tangerine is real, the person eating it is real. That is what it means to eat a tangerine in awareness.

"Children, what does it mean to eat a tangerine without awareness? When you are eating the tangerine, you do not know that you are eating the tangerine. You do not experience the lovely fragrance and sweet taste of the tangerine. When you peel the tangerine, you do not know that you are peeling the tangerine; when you remove a slice and put it in your mouth, you do not know that you are removing a slice and putting it in your mouth; when you smell the fragrance or taste the tangerine, you do not know that you are smelling the fragrance and tasting the tangerine. Eating a tangerine in such a way, you cannot appreciate its precious and wonderful nature. If you are not aware that you are eating the tangerine, the tangerine is not real. If the tangerine is not real, the person eating it is not real either. Children, that is eating a tangerine without awareness.

"Children, eating the tangerine in mindfulness means that while eating the tangerine you are truly in touch with it. Your mind is not chasing after thoughts of yesterday or tomorrow, but is dwelling fully in the present moment. The tangerine is truly present. Living in mindful awareness means to live in the present moment, your mind and body dwelling in the very here and now.

"A person who practices mindfulness can see things in the tangerine that others are unable to see. An aware person can see the tangerine tree, the tangerine blossom in the spring, the sunlight and rain which nourished the tangerine. Looking deeply, one can see ten thousand things which have made the tangerine possible. Looking at a tangerine, a person who practices awareness can see all the wonders of the universe and how all things interact with one another. Children, our daily life is just like a tangerine. Just as a tangerine is comprised of sections, each day is comprised of twenty-four hours. One hour is like one section of tangerine. Living all twenty-four hours of a day is like eating all the sections of a tangerine. The path I have found is the path of living each hour of the day in awareness, mind and body always dwelling in the present moment. The opposite is to live in forgetfulness. If we live in forgetfulness, we do not know that we are alive. We do not fully experience life because our mind and body are not dwelling in the here and now."

# Joseph Goldstein

## Exercise / Eating

*In the same way that the children learned, we too can experience being present as we eat. For your next meal, try this eating meditation by Vipassana teacher Joseph Goldstein.*

THERE ARE MANY different processes of mind and body which go on while we eat. It is important to become mindful of the sequence of the processes; otherwise, there is a great likelihood of greed and desire arising with regard to food. And when we are not aware, we do not fully enjoy the experience. We take a bite or two and our thoughts wander.

The first process involved when you have your food is that you see it. Notice "seeing, seeing." Then there is an intention to take the food, a mental process. That intention should be noticed. "Intending, intending." The mental intention becomes the cause of the arm moving. "Moving, moving." When the hand or spoon touches the food there is the sensation of touch, contact. Feel the sensations. Then the intention to lift the arm, and the lifting. Notice carefully all these processes.

Opening the mouth. Putting in the food. Closing the mouth. The intention to lower the arm, and then the movement. One thing at a time. Feeling the food in the mouth, the texture. Chewing. Experience the movement. As you begin chewing, there will be taste sensations arising. Be mindful of the tasting. As you keep on chewing, the taste disappears. Swallowing. Be aware of the whole sequence involved. There is no one behind it, no one who is eating. It's merely the sequence of intentions, movements, tastes, touch sensations. That's what we are—a sequence of happenings, of processes, and by being very mindful of the sequence, of the flow, we get free of the concept of self. We see this whole working of mind and body as a continuity of processes. Intentions, thoughts, sensations, movements, all in interrelationship to one another, the mind being the cause of bodily movements, bodily sensations being the cause of desires and intentions in the mind.

Usually we eat very unmindfully. Taste comes and goes very quickly. While food is still in the mouth, because of desire and greed for continuing taste sensations, the arm reaches for more, and generally we are unaware of the whole process involved. Finish each mouthful before reaching for another. In this way we become sensitive to our bodies and how much food

we need. It's very hard to overeat when you eat mindfully. . . . Incorporate the eating meditation into your
daily practice so there is no gap in the continuity of
awareness. From the moment you get up, through
everything done in the day, be very mindful, make it
all meditation.

# USING MANTRAS

The Sanskrit word mantra combines the root man ("to think")
with the suffix tra ("instrument" or "tool"). Therefore, mantra
means literally "tool for thinking." Since earliest Buddhist times,
the repetition of sacred phrases has been used as an aid for
meditation—to purify and focus the mind, to offer devotion or
thanks, or to protect and nurture the spiritual activity of a
particular person or place. Some authors differentiate between bijas,
or "seed syllables" (pure sounds such as om); mixed mantras, which
combine bijas with words that have translatable meanings; and
dharanis (phrases that are similar in function to mantras but can
be translated word for word).

Though some traditions lay claim to the ultimate mantra—the
one that includes or surpasses all others—in most cases such claims
can be taken simply as an expression of profound appreciation by
those who practice them.

# Lex Hixon

## *The Heart Sutra*

### GATE GATE PARAGATE PARASAMGATE BODHI SVAHA

O SHARIPUTRA, LISTEN CAREFULLY to these syl-
labic sounds which contain the entire Perfection of
Wisdom, as a vast tree is miraculously contained within a
small seed. This is the mantra which awakens every conscious stream into pure presence. This is the mantra of all
mantras, the mantra which transmits the principles of in-
comparability and inconceivability, the mantra which instantly dissipates the apparent darkness of egocentric miser,
the mantra which invokes only truth and does not acknowledge the separate self-existence of any falsehood: *gate gate
paragate parasamgate bodhi svaha* (gone, gone, gone beyond,
gone beyond even the beyond into full enlightenment, so
be it!).

# Patrul Rinpoche

## Mani

### OM MANI PADME HUM

THERE IS NO mantra that can be considered superior to the *mani*, which includes not only all the functions but also all the power and blessings of all other mantras. The learned sages of the past, like the great Karma Chagme, for example, were unable to find anywhere in the scriptures a mantra more beneficial, quintessential, or easier to practice than the *mani*; so it was this mantra that they took as their main practice. Even just hearing the *mani* can be enough to free beings from samsara. . . .

The *mani* is not just a string of ordinary words. It contains all the blessings and compassion of Chenrezi [the Bodhisattva of Compassion]; in fact, it is Chenrezi himself in the form of sound. As we are now, our karmic obscurations prevent us from being able to actually meet Chenrezi in his buddha-field; but what we can do is listen to his mantra, recite it, read it, and write it beautifully in golden letters. Since there is no difference between the deity himself and the mantra which is his essence, these activities bring great benefit. The six syllables are the expression of the six *paramitas* (virtues) of Chenrezi, and as he himself said, whoever recites the six-syllable mantra will perfect the six *paramitas* and purify all karmic obscurations. . . .

The sound of the mantra dispels ignorance and subdues all negative forces. It awakens the *shravakas* [arhats] from their meditative absorption and brings them to the Mahayana path; it makes offerings to the bodhisattvas, exhorting them to continue working for the benefit of beings; and it enjoins the dharma-protectors to safeguard the teachings and increase the happiness and prosperity of all.

The sounds of wind and running rivers, the crackling of fire, the cries of animals, the songs of birds, human voices—all the sounds of the universe—are the vibration of the six-syllable mantra, the self-arisen sound of the dharma, sound yet void, the resonance of the unborn *dharmakaya*. Through recitation, practicing the yoga of vajra speech, you will effortlessly attain the ordinary and supreme accomplishment.

# Nichirin Daishonin

## *The Lotus Sutra*

### NAM MYOHO RENGE KYO

SINCE THE *LOTUS* Sutra defines our life as the Buddha's life, our mind as the Buddha's wisdom, and our actions as the Buddha's behaviors, all who embrace and believe in even a single phrase or verse of this sutra will be endowed with these three properties. *Nam myoho renge kyo* is only one phrase, but it contains the essence of the entire sutra. . . .

The spirit within one's body may appear in just his face, and the spirit within his face may appear in just his eyes. Included within the word *Japan* is all that is within the country's sixty-six provinces: all of the people and animals, the rice paddies and other fields, those of high and low status, the nobles and the commoners, the seven kinds of gems, and all the other treasures. Similarly, included within the title *nam myoho renge kyo* is the entire sutra consisting of all eight volumes, twenty-eight chapters, and 69,384 characters without exception. Concerning this, Po-Chu-i stated that the title is to the sutra as eyes are to the Buddha. . . . Truly if you chant this in the morning and evening, you are correctly reading the entire *Lotus Sutra*. Chanting *daimoku* [great title] twice is the same as reading the entire sutra twice. . . . Thus if you ceaselessly chant *daimoku,* you will be continually reading the *Lotus Sutra*.

# Yoshinori Hiuga Sensei

## *Existence and Unity*

## NEMBUTSU

*NEMBUTSU* MEANS TO "meditate on the Buddha," though it usually refers to the Pure Land Buddhist practice of invoking the name of the Buddha through repetition of the mantra *namu amida butsu*. *Namu* is an expression of devotion meaning *praise* or *faith*, and *amida* is a Japanese epithet for the Buddha, combining the Sanskrit terms *amitayus* ("infinite life") and *amitabha* ("infinite light"). *Butsu* means "Buddha" in Japanese.

In nembutsu *samadhi* [meditative absorption]; logic and concepts do not exist. Nembutsu is the abandonment of self through chanting *namu amida butsu*—single-mindedly, devotedly, without becoming distracted by worldly thoughts or delusions. From within nembutsu, awakening arises. It comes to us from "the other shore."

Nembutsu means to meditate on the Amida Buddha who dwells in all things, and who also dwells in us. But that inner Buddha remains hidden in darkness until we become conscious of its presence.

When we become conscious of the inner *tathagata* ["thus gone one," the Buddha], it begins to govern our entire being, both mind and body, and to work through us. At first, illusion dominates us; ego rules upon the throne of our heart throughout the long journey of transmigration. But gradually we realize that all along, eternally, the Buddha has existed within us. With this realization, the Buddha ascends to the inner throne and begins to rule.

# Soen Nakagawa

## Everything Condensed

### NAMU DAI BOSA

THERE ARE MANY kinds of sutras, but all of them are condensed into this *namu dai bosa*. And this is condensed into *mu*; and this into *just zazen*. . . . Everything is condensed into this *namu dai bosa*. Not only the four-dimension world in which we human beings live—but also the five-, six- and endless-dimension worlds are all condensed into this *namu dai bosa*. This untouchable, unthinkable, universal world is each one of us; not only each one of us, but each of our cells. Do you know how many cells there are in your body? How many? I have never counted them myself, but a scholar has said there are seventeen billion cells in the human body. And, of course, in addition to these cells there are the electrons and other smaller elements—small, small, endlessly small . . . Each such thing—no matter how small—is a sentient being. This is the meaning of *dai*. As a character, *dai* [great] is usually considered the opposite of smallness. But since the true meaning of *dai* is absolute, in even the smallest thing there is this *dai*. *Bosa* you know; it means "enlightened one." Each of your cells is an enlightened one. Believe this! You are all such wonderful persons. This is Buddha. No need to say "Buddha." This is true— a true fact. This is not Zen; not Buddhism; not religious talk. It is just a plain fact. Right here, now—this is *namu dai bosa*. There is no need to think about endless-dimension universal worlds. Just *namu dai bosa*. Just *mu*. Just breathing. Just counting. Nothing else. Just . . . !

Some of you think zazen is difficult. It is. But on the other hand, it is very easy. The practice of zazen and chanting *namu dai bosa* is most easy. When you chant *namu dai bosa* you at once become a bodhisattva! . . . When I take your precious watch, I immediately become a thief; and if I were to kill you, I would at once become a murderer. All right? So when I chant *namu dai bosa,* I at once become a bodhisattva. It is *too* easy.

# LISTENING

*Creating the sounds in a mantra is one form of meditation. Another is to meditate on the sounds themselves. As Vipassana teacher Sylvia Boorstein observes, through meditating on sound we can experience the insight of impermanence.*

## Sylvia Boorstein

### Exercise / Sound Meditation

ONE SPECIFIC METHOD for practicing mindfulness of body sensations is to focus your attention on sounds. Sounds, like everything else, arise and pass away. Just by listening, you can experience the insight of impermanence, an understanding the Buddha taught as crucial for the development of wisdom.

Early morning is great for listening. Sounds start to slip into the stillness. In a rural setting, the sounds are likely to be those of birds and animals waking up. In a city, sounds of outside action begin—garbage collection, building construction, traffic. Even in the rarefied air of a high-rise hotel room, plumbing sounds and elevator sounds and footsteps in the hall pick up in pace.

Sit in a position in which you can be relaxed and

alert. Close your eyes. The stillness of your posture and the absence of visual stimuli both enhance hearing consciousness. People are sometimes surprised to discover how *much* sensory consciousness gets lost in the shuffle of distracted attention.

After your body is settled comfortably, just listen. Don't scan for sounds; wait for them. You might think of the difference between radar that goes out looking for something and a satellite dish with a wide range of pickup capacity that just sits in the backyard, waiting. Be a satellite dish. Stay turned on, but just wait.

At the beginning, you'll likely find that you are naming sounds: "door slam . . . elevator . . . footsteps . . . bird . . . airplane . . ." Sometimes you'll name the feeling tone that accompanies the experience: "bird pneumatic drill . . . unpleasant . . . laughter." After a while, you may discover that the naming impulse relaxes. What remains is awareness of the presence or absence of sounds: "hearing . . . not hearing . . . sound arising . . . sound passing away . . . pleasant . . . not pleasant."

Think of your listening meditation now as a wake-up exercise for your attention. However it happens— with names, without names, with feeling tone awareness or without—just let it happen. Don't try to accomplish anything. Just listen.

# VISUALIZATION

*Visualization involves not literal sight but rather the mental technique relying on the mind's eye. Tibetan Buddhist teacher Kathleen McDonald explores deepening meditation through "thinking in pictures," then guides us on a visualization of the body of light.*

## Kathleen McDonald

## *"Thinking" in Pictures*

IN YOUR ATTEMPTS to calm and concentrate your mind, you have probably noticed visual images among the many things that distract your attention from the object of meditation: faces of loved ones, your home, other familiar places, appetizing food, or memories of films you have seen. Such images arise spontaneously throughout the day but we are often too engrossed in external sensations to notice them. And each night our mind creates vivid scenes in which we interact with dream-people and dream-events. Visualization, or imagination, is thus a mental technique we are all familiar with, but unless our work lies in, say, art, design or film, we do little or nothing to develop and utilize it.

This natural capacity to think in pictures can be used to deepen our meditative experiences. Visualization is used in

several ways in the Tibetan tradition of spiritual development. It adds another dimension to analytical meditations—
for example, visualizing ourselves dying in order to sharpen
the awareness of our mortality. A mental image of the Buddha is recommended as the focus of attention in the development of single-pointed concentration, and visualizing
enlightened beings while praying helps to enhance our faith
and conviction.

But the art of visualization is used to its optimum in
Vajrayana, or tantra, the most profound and rapid means of
reaching enlightenment. The practices of this path involve
identifying oneself completely, body and mind, with an enlightened being and seeing one's environment as a pure
realm. The ordinary, mistaken perceptions of oneself and
all other phenomena are thus gradually abandoned as one's
potential for enlightenment is allowed to express itself.

The meditational deities visualized in Vajrayana practice,
such as Tara and Avalokiteshvara, are symbols of the enlightened state. Each is a manifestation of a specific quality.
Avalokiteshvara, for example, is the buddha of compassion
but each also represents the total experience of enlightenment. The details of the visualization, such as colors, im-
plements, hand gestures, posture and so forth, symbolize
different aspects of the path to spiritual fulfillment.

Meditation on these deities (or images from other
traditions that you are more comfortable with, for example,
Christ or Mary) helps us to open our hearts to the pure
energies of love, compassion, wisdom and strength that are

ever-present, all around us, wherever we may be. And, as the potential for these enlightened qualities lies within us, we should consider the images we contemplate to be reflections of our own true nature. Although ultimate reality is inexpressible, words lead us to discover it; so too can images remind us of the experience of enlightenment until it becomes a living reality.

The two kinds of meditation—analytical and stabilizing—are used together in visualization techniques. We need analytical thought to construct the image at the beginning of the meditation and to recall it whenever it is lost during the session. Analysis is also used to deal with other problems that might occur, such as distraction or negative thoughts.

But developing a clear visualization depends primarily on stabilizing meditation. Once the image has been established and we feel comfortable with it, we should hold it with single-pointed attention, not letting the mind be distracted to other objects. Initially, our concentration will last only a few seconds but with continual practice we will be able to maintain it for increasingly longer periods of time. Each time our attention wanders or we lose the object, we should again bring it to mind. This way of meditating both increases our familiarity with positive images and strengthens our ability to control and concentrate the mind.

It is common to find visualization difficult. If you are having problems, it could be that you are trying too hard or expecting too much. The mind needs to be in the right state—relaxed, clear and open. Too much effort creates tension, and the only vision that can appear is darkness. Too little concentration means the mind is crowded with distractions, leaving no space for a visualized image. We should learn to adjust our concentration as we would tune a musical instrument—with sensitivity and patience—until we have found the proper mental state in which the object can appear clearly.

Remember too that visualization utilizes only the *mental* faculty, not the eyes. If you find that you are straining to see something, you misunderstand the technique. Relax and let the image appear from within your mind.

Furthermore, we should be satisfied with whatever does appear, even if it is just a blur of color or a minor detail. It is more important to have a sense or feeling of the presence of an enlightened being than be too concerned about seeing a mental image. Thus it is very important to be relaxed and free of expectations. It is self-defeating to expect a complete, perfect visualization after one or two attempts; it may take years of practice before you can really see the image. Again, it is a matter of tuning the mind to the right balance; learning to work with the energies and elements of the mind to produce a positive, joyful meditative experience.

You might find it useful to practice visualization with familiar objects. Sit quietly with your eyes closed and bring to mind the image of a friend, for example. Try to see the details: the color and shape of the eyes, nose and mouth, the style of the hair, the shape of the body and so forth.

Experiment with other objects: your house, the view from your window, even your own face.

Visualizing deities is made easier by gazing at a picture or statue, then closing your eyes and trying to recall the image in detail. However, this helps you with the details only; don't think your visualized figure should be flat like a drawing or cold and lifeless like a statue. It should be warm, full of life and feeling, three-dimensional and made of pure, radiant light. Feel that you are actually in the presence of a blissful, compassionate, enlightened being.

Finally, it might be useful to practice the following simple visualization before attempting more complicated techniques.

# Kathleen McDonald

## Exercise / Body of Light Meditation

SIT COMFORTABLY, WITH your back straight, and breathe naturally. When your mind is calm and clear, visualize in the space above your head a sphere of white light, somewhat smaller than the size of your head, and pure, transparent and formless. Spend several minutes concentrating on the presence of the light. Don't worry if it does not appear sharply; it is enough just to feel it is there.

Contemplate that the sphere of light represents all universal goodness, love and wisdom: the fulfillment of your own highest potential. Then visualize that it decreases in size until it is about one inch in diameter and descends through the top of your head to your heart-center. From there it begins to expand once more, slowly spreading to fill your entire body. As it does, all the solid parts of your body dissolve and become light—your organs, bones, blood vessels, tissue and skin all become pure, formless white light.

Concentrate on the experience of your body as a body of light. Think that all problems, negativities and hindrances have completely vanished, and that you have reached a state of wholeness and perfection. Feel serene and joyful. If any thought or distracting object should appear in your mind, let it also dissolve into white light. Meditate in this way for as long as you can.

# FEELINGS AND METTA

*The Buddha encouraged meditating on the body as the body, the
mind as the mind, mind-objects as mind-objects, and feelings as
feelings. Awareness of negative feelings often seems more insistent
than recognition of positive feelings, so we'll begin with Thynn
Thynn's exploration of dealing with mental states in daily life.
Some of the earliest Buddhist concentration practices in fact began
with focusing on loving kindness, or metta, so after considering
Joseph Goldstein's observations on training of the heart, we'll turn
to Sharon Salzberg's guidance into metta practice.*

## Thynn Thynn

### Attention to Emotions

WHEN YOU SPEAK of meditation, you may think of
the type of meditation that is popular these days, the
sitting form of meditation. But that form is merely an aid,
a support to develop a mental discipline of mindfulness and
equanimity. The form should not be mistaken for the path.

The popular notion is that you need to set aside a special
time or place to meditate. In actuality, if meditation is to
help you acquire peace of mind as you function in your life,
then it must be a dynamic activity, part and parcel of your
daily experience. Meditation is here and now, moment-to-

moment, amid the ups and downs of life, amid conflicts, disappointments and heartaches—amid success and stress. If you want to understand and resolve anger, desires, attachments and all the myriad emotions and conflicts, need you go somewhere else to find the solution? If your house was on fire, you wouldn't go somewhere else to put out the fire, would you?

If you really want to understand your mind, you must watch it while it is angry, while it desires, while it is in conflict. You must pay attention to the mind as the one-thousand-and-one thoughts and emotions rise and fall. The moment you pay attention to your emotions, you will find that they lose their strength and eventually die out. However, when you are inattentive, you find that these emotions go on and on. Only after the anger has subsided are you aware that you have been angry. By then, either you have made some unwanted mistakes or you have ended up emotionally drained. . . .

To understand the mind, you have to watch and pay attention with an uncluttered, silent mind. When your mind is chattering away, all the time asking questions, then it lacks the capacity to look. It is too busy asking questions, answering, asking.

Try to experience watching yourself in silence. That silence is the silence of the mind free from discriminations, free from likes and dislikes, free from clinging.

Only when your mind is free from clinging and rejecting can it see anger as anger, desire as desire. As soon as you "see" your mental process is fully preoccupied with "seeing," and in that split second anger dies a natural death. This seeing, or insight, called *panna,* arises as a spontaneous awareness that can be neither practiced nor trained. This awareness brings new insight into life, new clarity and new spontaneity in action.

So, you see, meditation need not be separate from life and its daily ups and downs. If you are to experience peace in this everyday world, you need to watch, understand and deal with your anger, desire and ignorance as they occur. Only when you cease to be involved with your emotions can the peaceful nature of your mind emerge. This peace-nature enables you to live every moment of your life completely. With this newfound understanding and awareness, you can live as a complete individual with greater sensitivity. You will come to view life with new and fresh perceptions. Strangely enough, what you saw as problems before are problems no more.

# Joseph Goldstein

## *Training of the Heart*

THERE HAS BEEN an interesting discussion over the last twenty-five hundred years about where consciousness resides. Does it reside in the brain? Does it reside in the heart?

Without trying to provide a definitive answer to that question, I think it is useful at least to know that at times in meditative experience there can be a very strong sense of consciousness emanating from the heart center—not the physical heart, but rather the psychic energy center in the middle of the chest. It may be that the energy of consciousness comes from the brain and is felt at the heart, or perhaps it starts at the heart center and is processed through the brain.

Some Asian languages resolve this issue quite naturally by using exactly the same word for both heart and mind. When we say "mind" in the Buddhist sense, we do not mean just the brain or the intellect. "Mind" in this sense means consciousness: the knowing faculty, that which knows an object, along with all of the mental and emotional feeling states associated with that knowing, states that can arise in different combinations in any particular moment. So in this meditative understanding, mind and heart are really the same thing.

What, then, is the training of the heart, the transformation of consciousness? Consciousness is simply knowing. But along with each moment of knowing, different associated mental states may arise. The teachings have a lot to say about these states—unwholesome ones like greed, hatred, fear, and delusion; and wholesome ones such as mindfulness, compassion, love, and wisdom.

We can understand the training of the heart as being what the Buddha called "the four great efforts": In our practice we make the effort to diminish the unwholesome mental states that have already arisen, and to prevent those that have not yet arisen from arising. And conversely, we make the effort to strengthen those wholesome mental states that are already developed, and to cultivate and develop the wholesome states that have not yet arisen.

This, then, is the formula for transformation. First we take a close look at this heart-mind to see what is what. Through the careful practice of looking, we develop a discriminating wisdom, so that we understand for ourselves what mental states are unskillful, that is, leading to suffering, and what states are skillful, leading to happiness. And based on our own experience, our own clear seeing, we begin to arouse these four great efforts. This is the training of the heart in which we are engaged.

# Sharon Salzberg

## *Metta Practice*

IN DOING METTA practice, we gently repeat phrases that are meaningful in terms of what we wish, first for ourselves and then for others. We begin by befriending ourselves. The aspirations we articulate should be deeply felt and somewhat enduring (not something like "May I find a good show on television tonight"). Classically there are four phrases used:

"May I be free from danger."

"May I have mental happiness."

"May I have physical happiness."

"May I have ease of well-being."

I will describe these phrases here in detail, and you can experiment with them, alter them, or simply choose an alternative set of three or four phrases. Discover personally in your own heartfelt investigation what is truly significant for you.

*"May I be free from danger."* We begin to extend care and lovingkindness toward ourselves with the wish that we may find freedom from danger, that we may know safety. We ultimately wish that all beings as well as ourselves have a sense of refuge, have a safe haven, have freedom from internal torment and external violence.

There is a nightmarish quality to life without safety. When we live repeatedly lost in conditioned states such as anger and greed, continually being hurt and hurting others, there is no peace or safety. When we are awakened at night by anxiety, guilt, and agitation—there is no peace or safety. When we live in a world of overt violence, which rests on the disempowerment of people and the loneliness of unspoken and silenced abuse—there is no peace or safety. This deep aspiration is the traditional beginning. "May I be free from danger." Other possible phrases are "May I have safety" and "May I be free from fear."

*"May I have mental happiness."* If we were in touch with our own loveliness, if we felt less fearful of others, if we trusted our ability to love, we would have mental happiness. In the same vein, if we could relate skillfully to the torments of the mind that arise, and not nourish or cultivate them, we would have mental happiness. Even in very positive or fortunate circumstances, without mental happiness, we are miserable. Sometimes people use the phrase "May I be happy" or "May I be peaceful" or "May I be liberated."

*"May I have physical happiness."* With this phrase we wish ourselves the enjoyment of health, freedom from physical pain, and harmony with our bodies. If freedom from pain is not a realistic possibility, we aspire to receive the pain with friendliness and patience, thereby not transforming physical pain into mental torment. You might also use a phrase such as "May I be healthy," "May I be healed," "May I make a friend of my body," or "May I embody my love and understanding."

*"May I have ease of well-being."* This phrase points to the exigencies of everyday life—concerns such as relationships, family issues, and livelihood. With the expression of this phrase we wish that these elements of our day-to-day lives be free from struggle, that they be accomplished gracefully, and easily. Alternative phrases could be "May I live with ease" or "May lovingkindness manifest throughout my life" or "May I dwell in peace."

# Sharon Salzberg

## *Exercise / Lovingkindness*

SIT COMFORTABLY. YOU can begin with five minutes of reflection on the good within you or your wish to be happy. Then choose three or four phrases that express what you most deeply wish for yourself, and repeat them over and over again. You can coordinate the phrases with the breath, if you wish, or simply have your mind rest in the phrases without a physical anchor. Feel free to experiment, and be creative. Without trying to force or demand a loving feeling, see if there are circumstances you can imagine yourself in where you can more readily experience friendship with yourself. Is it seeing yourself as a young child? One friend imagined himself sitting surrounded by all the most loving people he had ever heard of in the world, receiving their kindness and good wishes.

For the first time, love for himself seemed to enter his heart.

Develop a gentle pacing with the phrases; there is no need to rush through them, or say them harshly. You are offering yourself a gift with each phrase. If your attention wanders, or if difficult feelings or memories arise, try to let go of them in the spirit of kindness, and begin again repeating the metta phrases:

"May I be free from danger."

"May I have mental happiness."

"May I have physical happiness."

"May I have ease of well-being."

There are times when feelings of unworthiness come up strongly, and you clearly see the conditions that limit your love for yourself. Breathe gently, accept that these feelings have arisen, remember the beauty of your wish to be happy, and return to the metta phrases.

# PROBLEMS IN MEDITATING

## Sogyal Rinpoche

### The Mind's Own Radiance

*In our training of the mind and heart, we often experience our thoughts and emotions running wild. As uncomfortable as mental and emotional distractions may be, Tibetan teacher Sogyal Rinpoche observes that this "riot" is an inevitable part of our meditation experience, which we learn to transform as we grow quieter in the process.*

WHEN PEOPLE BEGIN to meditate, they often say that their thoughts are running riot, and have become wilder than ever before. But I reassure them and say that this is a good sign. Far from meaning that your thoughts have become wilder, it shows that you have become quieter, and you are finally aware of just how noisy your thoughts have always been. Don't be disheartened or give up. Whatever arises, just keep being present, keep returning to the breath, even in the midst of all the confusion.

In the ancient meditation instructions it is said that at the beginning thoughts will arrive one on top of another, uninterrupted, like a steep mountain waterfall. Gradually, as you perfect meditation, thoughts become like the water in a deep, narrow gorge, then a great river slowly winding its way down to the sea, and finally the mind becomes like a still and placid ocean, ruffled by only the occasional ripple or wave.

Sometimes people think that when they meditate there should be no thoughts and emotions at all—and when thoughts and emotions do arise, they become annoyed and exasperated with themselves and think they have failed. Nothing could be further from the truth. There is a Tibetan saying: "It's a tall order to ask for meat without bones, and tea without leaves." So long as you have a mind, there will be thoughts and emotions.

Just as the ocean has waves, or the sun has rays, so the mind's own radiance is its thoughts and emotions. The ocean has waves, yet the ocean is not particularly disturbed by them. The waves are the very nature of the ocean. Waves will rise, but where do they go? Back into the ocean. And where do the waves come from? The ocean. In the same manner, thoughts and emotions are the radiance and expression of the very nature of the mind. They rise from the mind, but where do they dissolve? Back into the mind. Whatever rises, do not see it as a particular problem. If you do not impulsively react, if you are only patient, it will once again settle into its essential nature.

When you have this understanding, then rising thoughts only enhance your practice. But when you do not understand what they intrinsically are—the radiance of the nature

of your mind—then your thoughts become the seed of confusion. So have a spacious, open, and compassionate attitude
toward your thoughts and emotions, because in fact your
thoughts are your family, the family of your mind. Before
them, as Dudjom Rinpoche used to say: "Be like an old
wise man, watching a child play."

# The Buddha

## *Maha-Assapura Sutta*

*When our thoughts and emotions are at play, distracting us, they most often fall within one of five large categories known as the hindrances: desire, aversion, sloth and torpor, restlessness, and doubt. Teachers from the Buddha to Joseph Goldstein have recognized these "enemies" and the need to deal with them.*

" . . . HERE, BHIKKHUS, A bhikkhu resorts to a secluded resting place: the forest, the root of a tree, a mountain, a ravine, a hillside cave, a charnel ground, a jungle thicket, an open space, a heap of straw.

"On returning from his almsround, after his meal he sits down, folding his legs crosswise, setting his body erect and establishing mindfulness before him. Abandoning covetousness for the world, he abides with a mind free from covetousness; he purifies his mind from covetousness. Abandoning ill will and hatred, he abides with a mind free from ill will, compassionate for the welfare of all living beings; he purifies his mind from ill will and hatred. Abandoning sloth and torpor, he abides free from sloth and torpor, percipient of light, mindful and fully aware; he purifies his mind from sloth and torpor. Abandoning restlessness and remorse, he abides unagitated with a mind inwardly peaceful; he purifies his mind from restlessness and remorse. Abandoning doubt, he abides having gone beyond doubt, unperplexed about wholesome states; he purifies his mind from doubt.

"Bhikkhus, suppose a man were to take a loan and undertake business and his business were to succeed so that he could repay all the money of the old loan and there would remain enough extra to maintain a wife; then on considering this, he would be glad and full of joy. Or suppose a man were afflicted, suffering and gravely ill, and his food would not agree with him and his body had no strength, but later he would recover from the affliction and his food would agree with him and his body would regain strength; then on considering this, he would be glad and full of joy. Or suppose a man were imprisoned in a prison-house, but later he would be released from prison, safe and secure, with no loss to his property; then on considering this, he would be glad and full of joy. Or suppose a man were a slave, not self-dependent but dependent on others, unable to go where he wants, but later on he would be released from slavery, self-dependent, independent of others, a freed man able to go where he wants; then on considering this, he would be glad and full of joy. Or suppose a man with wealth and property were to enter a road across a desert, but later on he would cross over the desert, safe and secure, with no loss to his property; then on considering this, he would be glad and full of joy. So too, bhikkhus, when these five hindrances are unabandoned in himself, a bhikkhu sees them respectively as a debt, a disease, a prisonhouse, slavery, and a road across a desert. But when these five hindrances have been abandoned in himself, he sees that as freedom from debt, healthiness, release from prison, freedom from slavery, and a land of safety.''

# Joseph Goldstein

## The Hindrances

IMAGINE YOURSELVES IN the middle of a battlefield, single-handedly facing a thousand enemies. Though surrounded on all sides, you somehow manage to conquer them. Imagine yourself on this battlefield a thousand different times, and each time you overcome the enemies around you. The Buddha has said that this is an easier task than the conquering of oneself. It is not a trivial thing we have set about doing. The most difficult of all possible tasks is to come to understand one's own mind. But it is not impossible. There have been many beings who have conquered these thousand enemies a thousand times, and they have given us advice and guidance.

The first big help is to recognize who the enemies are. Unrecognized, they remain powerful forces in the mind; in the light of recognition, they become much easier to deal with. There are five powerful enemies in the battlefield of the mind and learning to recognize them is essential in penetrating to deeper levels of understanding.

The first of these enemies, or hindrances, is sense desire: lusting after sense pleasure, grasping at sense objects. It keeps the mind looking outward, searching after this object or that, in an agitated and unbalanced way. It is in the very nature of sense desires that they can never be satisfied. There is no end to the seeking. We enjoy a pleasurable object, it arises and disappears, as do all phenomena, and we are left with the same unsatiated desire for more gratification. Until we deal with that kind of grasping in the mind we remain always unfulfilled, always seeking a new pleasure, a new delight. It can be desires for beautiful sights, beautiful sounds, tastes or smells, pleasant sensations in the body, or fascinating ideas. Attachment to these objects strengthens the greed factor; and it is precisely greed in the mind, this clinging and grasping, which keeps us bound on the wheel of samsara, the wheel of life and death. Until we deal successfully with the hindrance of sense desire, we stay bound by the forces of attachment and possessiveness.

The second enemy is hatred; anger, ill will, aversion, annoyance, irritation, are all expressions of the condemning mind. It is the mind which strikes against the object and wants to get rid of it. It is a very turbulent and violent state. In English we use two expressions which clearly indicate the effect of these two enemies, sense desire and ill will. We say a person is "burning with desire," or a person is "burning up," to mean he or she is very angry. The mind in these states is literally burning: a great deal of suffering.

The third enemy is sloth and torpor, which means laziness of mind, sluggishness. A mind that is filled with sloth and torpor wants just to go to sleep. There is an animal called a slug which has always represented to me this quality of sloth and torpor: it barely inches along, rather unenergetically. Unless we overcome that kind of drowsiness and sluggishness of mind, nothing gets done, nothing is seen clearly, our mind remains heavy and dull.

The fourth hindrance is restlessness. A mind that is in a state of worry, regret, and agitation is unable to stay concentrated. It is always jumping from one object to another, without any mindfulness. This unsettledness of mind prevents the arising of deep insight.

The fifth of the great enemies is doubt, and in some ways it is the most difficult of all. Until we see through it, doubt incapacitates the mind, blocking our effort for clarity. Doubt arises about what one is doing and about one's ability to do it. . . .

All of these hindrances—desire, anger, sloth and torpor, restlessness, doubt—are mental factors. They are not self, just impersonal factors functioning in their own way. A simile is given to illustrate the effect of these different obstructions in the mind. Imagine a pond of clear water. Sense desire is like the water becoming colored with pretty dyes. We become entranced with the beauty and intricacy of the color and so do not penetrate to the depths. Anger, ill will, aversion, is like boiling water. Water that is boiling is very turbulent. You can't see through to the bottom. This kind of turbulence in the mind, the violent reaction of hatred and aversion, is a great obstacle to understanding. Sloth and torpor is like the pond of water covered with algae, very dense. One cannot possibly penetrate to the bottom because you can't see through the algae. It is a very heavy mind. Restlessness and worry are like a pond when wind-swept. The surface of the water is agitated by strong winds. When influenced by restlessness and worry, insight becomes impossible because the mind is not centered or calm. Doubt is like the water when muddied; wisdom is obscured by murkiness and cloudiness.

There are specific ways to deal with these enemies as they confront us on the path. The first is to recognize them, to see them clearly in each moment. If sense desire arises, to know immediately that there is desire in the mind, or if there is anger, or sloth, or restlessness, or doubt, to recognize immediately the particular obstacle that has arisen. That very recognition is the most powerful, most effective way of overcoming them. Recognition leads to mindfulness. And mindfulness means not clinging, not condemning, not identifying with the object. All the hindrances are impermanent mental factors. They arise and they pass away, like clouds in the sky. If we are mindful of them when they arise and don't react or identify with them, they pass through the mind, without creating any disturbance. Mindfulness is the most effective way of dealing with them.

There are also specific antidotes to these hindrances when the mind becomes somewhat overpowered by them and mindfulness is still weak. When sense desire overcomes the mind, it is good to reflect upon the true nature of this decaying body, the fact that we are all going to end as corpses. In what may seem just a moment's time, we will be seventy or eighty or ninety years old. . . . This kind of reflection weakens lust as we realize the imminence of our own death. It's not that death is for some and not for others. We do not feel the uniqueness and power of the moment when we do not feel the urgency of our death.

There is also a strong correlation between the degree of desire we experience and over-indulgence in food and sleep. Moderation in eating and sleeping weakens the factor of desire and brings greater clarity.

Ill will, anger, aversion, hatred; again, the best way of dealing with these hindrances is to be aware of them, to be mindful. You are sitting and all of a sudden are filled with ill will towards a person or situation. Sit back and notice, "anger, anger." Not identifying with it, not condemning oneself for being angry. Simply watch. It arises and passes away. Anger is strong when it is fed with identification, "I'm angry and I should be angry because someone did something to me . . ." As an alternative to the indulgence of expressing ill will, just closely observe it. You will find that it loses its power to disturb the mind. A specific way of dealing with ill will when it is too overpowering is to generate loving thoughts: wishing happiness and love to all beings everywhere, to individual people you feel very kindly towards, and finally to the specific person you may be angry at, surrounding that person with loving thoughts even though at the time it may be difficult. Slowly the anger will dissipate and the mind will again become cool and balanced. A very practical way of dealing with ill will, if you are feeling very strong aversion towards someone, is to give them a gift. It is hard to stay angry in the act of giving and, because you are being generous and open, it helps to dissolve the tensions and irritations that were there. It is a skillful way of freeing the mind from the fire of hatred.

Perhaps an even more insightful way of dealing with anger and aversion is to reflect upon the law of karma: to understand that we are all the heirs of our own actions. Every being is going to experience the results of his wholesome and unwholesome deeds. If somebody is doing something unwholesome, instead of reacting with anger, we can respond with compassion, understanding that the person is acting out of ignorance, in a way that will bring back pain and suffering to himself. There is no need to add to the suffering he is causing for himself; rather, out of compassion, we should try to ease that burden of ignorance.

Sloth and torpor. Again, the very best way of dealing with it is to observe it carefully, examining and investigating the qualities of sloth and torpor and sluggishness in the mind. Penetrate into it. With this kind of investigating mindfulness you can often experience all the sleepiness, all the drowsiness disappearing in just a moment. You can be noticing for some time "sleepy, sleepy," and then in a moment, the mind will become fully awake and mindful. By paying attention and not identifying with the feeling of sleepiness, it will usually pass away. But if you try being mindful and keep nodding off anyway, there are some specific things to do. Change posture. If you're sitting, get up and do some brisk walking. Or if you're inside, go outside. Being in the fresh air energizes one again. Look at a light for a few moments, either an electric light, moonlight, or starlight. The effect of light awakens the system. Throw cold water on yourself. Try walking backwards. Sloth and torpor are impermanent and can be overcome. If you have done all these things and are still nodding off, then it is time to go to sleep. But make the effort. If every time drowsiness comes into the mind we think, "Oh well, I'll take a little nap," it makes the factor of sloth stronger. Be resolute and energetic in dealing with this hindrance.

Restlessness and agitation. Again, be mindful of it. Look at the restless mind, examine what that mind is all about, pay close attention to the quality of restlessness. If you're sitting and are feeling agitated and not concentrated, make that mental state the object of awareness. Just sit and watch, "restless, restless." Observe without identifying with it. There is no "one" who is restless; rather it is the working of a particular mental factor. It comes and goes. If there is a balanced awareness, it does not disturb the mind.

Another way is to make the effort to concentrate the mind, to make the mind one-pointed. This is the specific antidote to restlessness. If the mind is feeling very agitated, return to the awareness of the breath. Give the mind a single object and stay with that object for a period of time, twenty minutes, half an hour, so that the factor of concentration becomes strong again. Sitting motionless in a very straight and precise posture also helps to overcome restlessness.

The last of the enemies is doubt. It is essential to see what doubt is all about because it can be an impenetrable barrier on the path. One just gives up. Again, the most effective and insightful way of dealing with doubt is to look at it, to face it, to acknowledge it. When doubt is present, pay full attention to the doubting mind, without identifying with it. Doubt is not self, not mine, and not I. It is merely a thought, a mental factor. If we can see it and not identify with it, the doubt comes, we sit back and notice, "doubting, doubting," and it goes away.

Another way of dealing with doubt is to have a good conceptual understanding of what it is that we're doing, what the whole path of insight is about. There is no need for any kind of blind faith or acceptance. Understanding the Dharma on the intellectual level can be a great help in resolving doubts as they arise. Then when doubt comes you are able to clarify it from your own experience, your own understanding.

Often there is a tendency to condemn the hindrances when they arise. The condemning mind is itself the factor of aversion. Every act of condemning the hindrances strengthens the enemy. That's not the way. No judging, no evaluating. The hindrances come, simply observe them. Mindfulness makes them all inoperative. They may continue to arise, but they do not disturb the mind because we are not reacting to them.

As long as the hindrances remain strong in the mind, it is difficult to develop insight and wisdom. . . . The difficulties at the beginning are not the enemies' last stand. They will arise again as the mind begins to penetrate into deeper levels of conditioning. But now there should be some confidence in your ability to deal with these factors, having seen them come and go, arise and vanish. The understanding that they are impermanent gives a strong balance to the mind. Please sustain the effort and continuity of awareness; the mind which has overcome the power of the hindrances is quite unshakable in its balance and pliability.

# Hakuin Yasutani Roshi

## Counting Breaths

*Many teachers find that the simplest way to refocus the mind is to
return to the breath and count the inhalations. Zen master Hakuin
Yasutani describes counting without trying to stop consciousness, but
without pursuing the perceptions and sensations that arise.*

THERE ARE MANY good methods of concentration be-
queathed to us by our predecessors in Zen. The easiest
for beginners is counting incoming and outgoing breaths.
The value of this particular exercise lies in the fact that all
reasoning is excluded and the discriminative mind put at
rest. Thus the waves of thought are stilled and a gradual
one-pointedness of mind achieved. To start with, count both
inhalations and exhalations. When you inhale concentrate
on "one"; when you exhale, on "two"; and soon, up to
ten. Then you return to "one" and once more count up
to ten, continuing as before. If you lose the count, return
to "one." It is as simple as that.

Fleeting thoughts which naturally fluctuate in the mind
are not in themselves an impediment. This unfortunately is
not commonly recognized. Even among Japanese who have

been practicing Zen for five years or more there are many who misunderstand Zen practice to be a stopping of consciousness. There is indeed a kind of zazen meditation that aims at doing just this, but it is not the traditional zazen of Zen Buddhism. You must realize that no matter how intently you count your breaths you will still perceive what is in your line of vision, since your eyes are open, and you will hear the normal sounds about you, as your ears are not plugged. And since your brain likewise is not asleep, various thought forms will dart about in your mind. Now, they will not hamper or diminish the effectiveness of zazen unless, evaluating them as "good," you cling to them or, deciding they are "bad," you try to check or eliminate them. You must not regard any perceptions or sensations as an obstruction to zazen, nor should you pursue any of them. I emphasize this. "Pursuit" simply means that in the act of seeing, your gaze lingers on objects; in the course of hearing, your attention dwells on sounds; and in the process of thinking, your mind adheres to ideas. If you allow yourself to be distracted in such ways, your concentration on the counting of your breaths will be impeded. To recapitulate: let random thoughts arise and vanish as they will, do not dally with them and do not try to expel them, but merely concentrate all your energy on counting the inhalations and exhalations of your breath.

# Venerable Henepola Gunaratana

## When the Mind Wanders

*Sometimes simply counting breaths does not stop the mind from wandering. Theravadan teacher Venerable Henepola Gunaratana suggests five alternative ways of counting breaths and gives tips that can help us come back to our breath so that we may balance energy, faith, mindfulness, concentration, and wisdom.*

IN SPITE OF your concerted effort to keep the mind on your breathing, the mind may wander away. It may go to past experiences and suddenly you may find yourself remembering places you've visited, people you met, friends not seen for a long time, a book you read long ago, the taste of food you ate yesterday, and so on. As soon as you notice that your mind is no longer on your breath, mindfully bring it back and anchor it there. However, in a few moments you may be caught up again thinking how to pay your bills, to make a telephone call to your friend, write a letter to someone, do your laundry, buy your groceries, go to a party, plan your next vacation, and so forth. As soon as you notice that your mind is not on your object, bring it back mindfully. Following are some suggestions to help you gain the concentration necessary for the practice of mindfulness.

## 1. COUNTING

In a situation like this, counting may help. The purpose of counting is simply to focus the mind on the breath. Once your mind is focused on the breath, give up counting. This is a device for gaining concentration. There are numerous ways of counting. Any counting should be done mentally. Do not make any sound when you count. Following are some of the ways of counting.

a. While breathing in, count "one, one, one, one . . ." until the lungs are full of fresh air. While breathing out count "two, two, two, two . . ." until the lungs are empty of fresh air. Then while breathing in again count "three, three, three, three, three . . ." until the lungs are full again and while breathing out count again "four, four, four, four . . ." until the lungs are empty of fresh air. Count up to ten and repeat as many times as necessary to keep the mind focused on the breath.

b. The second method of counting is counting rapidly up to ten. While counting "one, two, three, four, five, six, seven, eight, nine and ten," breathe in, and again while counting "one, two, three, four, five, six, seven, eight, nine and ten," breathe out. This means that with one inhalation you should count up to ten and with one exhalation you should count up to ten. Repeat this way of counting as many times as necessary to focus the mind on the breath.

c. The third method of counting is to count in succession up to ten. At this time, count "one, two, three, four, five" (only up to five) while inhaling and then count "one, two, three, four, five, six" (up to six) while exhaling. Again, count "one, two, three, four, five, six, seven" (only up to seven) while inhaling. Then count "one, two, three, four, five, six, seven, eight" while exhaling. Count up to nine while inhaling and count up to ten while exhaling. Repeat this way of counting as many times as necessary to focus the mind on the breath.

d. The fourth method is to take a long breath. When the lungs are full, mentally count "one" and breathe out completely until the lungs are empty of fresh air. Then count mentally "two." Take a long breath again and count "three" and breathe out completely as before. When the lungs are empty of fresh air, count mentally "four." Count your breath in this manner up to ten. Then count backward from ten to one. Count again from one to ten and then ten to one.

e. The fifth method is to join inhaling and exhaling. When the lungs are empty of fresh air, count mentally "one." This time you should count both inhalation and exhalation as one. Again inhale, exhale, and mentally count "two." This way of counting should be done only up to five and repeated from five to one. Repeat this method until your breathing becomes refined and quiet.

Remember that you are not supposed to continue your counting all the time. As soon as your mind is locked at the nostril-tip where the inhalation and exhalation touch and you begin to feel that your breathing is so refined and quiet that you cannot notice inhalation and exhalation separately, you should give up counting. Counting is used only to train the mind to concentrate on one object.

## 2. CONNECTING

After inhaling do not wait to notice the brief pause before exhaling but connect the inhaling with exhaling, so you can notice both inhaling and exhaling as one continuous breath.

## 3. FIXING

After joining inhaling with exhaling, fix your mind on the point where you feel your inhaling and exhaling breath touching. Inhale and exhale as one single breath moving in and out touching or rubbing the rims of your nostrils.

## 4. FOCUS YOUR MIND LIKE A CARPENTER

A carpenter draws a straight line on a board that he wants to cut. Then he cuts the board with his saw along the straight line he drew. He does not look at the teeth of his saw as they move in and out of the board. Rather he focuses his entire attention on the line he drew so he can cut the board straight. Similarly, keep your mind straight on the point where you feel the breath at the rims of your nostrils.

## 5. MAKE YOUR MIND LIKE A GATEKEEPER

A gatekeeper does not take into account any detail of the people entering a house. All he does is notice people entering the house and leaving the house through the gate. Similarly, when you concentrate you should not take into account any detail of your experiences. Simply notice the feeling of your inhaling and exhaling breath as it goes in and out right at the rims of your nostrils.

As you continue your practice your mind and body become so light that you may feel as if you are floating in the air or on water. You may even feel that your body is springing up into the sky. When the grossness of your in-

and-out breathing has ceased, subtle in-and-out breathing arises. This very subtle breath is your mind's object of focus. This is the sign of concentration. This first appearance of a sign-object will be replaced by a more and more subtle sign-object. This subtlety of the sign can be compared to the sound of a bell. When a bell is struck with a big iron rod, you hear a gross sound at first. As the sound fades away, the sound becomes very subtle. Similarly, the in-and-out breath appears at first as a gross sign. As you keep paying bare attention to it, this sign becomes very subtle. But the consciousness remains totally focused on the rims of the nostrils. Other meditation objects become clearer and clearer, as the sign develops. But the breath becomes subtler and subtler as the sign develops. Because of this subtlety, you may not notice the presence of your breath. Don't get disappointed thinking that you lost your breath or that nothing is happening to your meditation practice. Don't worry. Be mindful and determined to bring your feeling of breath back to the rims of your nostrils. This is the time you should practice more vigorously, balancing your energy, faith, mindfulness, concentration, and wisdom.

# Jack Kornfield

## *Exercise / Hindrances*

*All of our experiences in everyday life become part of our practice,
even the hindrances that arise when we are meditating. Vipassana
teacher Jack Kornfield invites us to make the hindrances part
of our path.*

CHOOSE ONE OF the most frequent and difficult mind states that arise in your practice, such
as irritation, fear, boredom, lust, doubt, or restlessness. For one week in your daily sitting be particularly
aware each time this state arises. Watch carefully for
it. Notice how it begins and what precedes it. Notice
if there is a particular thought or image that triggers
this state. Notice how long it lasts and when it ends.
Notice what state usually follows it. Observe whether
it ever arises very slightly or softly. Can you see it as
just a whisper in the mind? See how loud and strong
it gets. Notice what patterns of energy or tension reflect this state in the body. Become aware of any physical or mental resistance to experiencing this state.

Soften and receive even the resistance. Finally sit and be aware of the breath, watching and waiting for this state, allowing it to come, and observing it like an old friend.

# Postscript

## Jon Kabat-Zinn

### *Keeping It Simple*

IF YOU DO decide to start meditating, there's no need to tell other people about it, or talk about why you are doing it or what it's doing for you. In fact, there's no better way to waste your nascent energy and enthusiasm for practice and thwart your efforts so they will be unable to gather momentum. Best to meditate without advertising it.

Every time you get a strong impulse to talk about meditation and how wonderful it is, or how hard it is, or what it's doing for you these days, or what it's not, or you want to convince someone else how wonderful it would be for them, just look at it as more thinking and go meditate some more. The impulse will pass and everybody will be better off—especially you.

# Buddhist Meditation and Study Centers

Throughout the United States, the number of Buddhist centers for study and meditation has been growing rapidly. Those listed below exist at the time of this writing and are included only to help you find a center in your area. Many of the centers have newsletters that can give you information about sponsored events, and *Tricycle* magazine carries in each issue a listing of centers and other resources.

## Northeast

**Living Dharma Center**
[Zen]
PO Box 304
Amherst, MA 01004
413-259-1611

**Barre Center for Buddhist Studies** [Mixed traditions]
149 Lockwood Road
Barre, MA 01005
508-355-2347

**Insight Meditation Society** [Vipassana]
1230 Pleasant Street
Barre, MA 01005
508-355-4378

**Kurukulla Center** [Tibetan]
Astor Station, PO Box 268
Boston, MA 02123-0268
617-421-9668

**Boston Jodo Mission**
[Pure Land]
296 East Eighth Street #3
Boston, MA 02127
617-269-7807

**Cambridge Insight Meditation Center**
[Vipassana]
331 Broadway
Cambridge, MA 02138
617-491-5070

**Cambridge Zen Center**
[Zen]
199 Auburn Street
Cambridge, MA 02139
617-576-3229

**Center for the Awareness of Pattern** [Soto Zen]
PO Box 407
Freeport, ME 04032
207-865-3396

**Morgan Bay Zendo**
[Mixed traditions]
PO Box 188
Surry, ME 04684
207-374-9963

**Barrington Zen Center**
7 Lois Lane
Barrington, NH 03825
603-664-7654

**FWBO Aryloka Retreat
Center**
14 Heartwood Circle
Newmarket, NH 03857

**Milarepa Center** [Tibetan]
Barnet Mountain
Barnet, VT 05821
802-633-4136

**Zen Affiliate of VT**
VT Affiliate of Zen Mountain
Monastery
802-658-6466
(Burlington)
802-229-0164
(Montpelier)
802-228-2476
(Springfield)

**Providence Zen Center**
99 Pound Road
Cumberland, RI 02864
401-658-1476

**Living Dharma Center**
[Zen]
PO Box 513
Bolton, CT 06043
203-742-7049

**Mandala Buddhist Center**
[Shingon]
RR 1, Box 2380
Bristol, VT 05443
802-453-5038

**Mindfulness Sangha**
255 Cherry Street
New Britain, CT 06051
860-612-0077

**Karmê-Chöling Buddhist
and Shambala
Meditation Center**
[Tibetan]
Barnet, VT 05821
802-633-2384

**New Haven Shambhala
Center** [Tibetan]
319 Peck Streeet
New Haven, CT 06513
203-776-2331

**Center for Dzogchen
Studies** [Nyingma/Kagyu]
847 Whalley Avenue
New Haven, CT 06515
203-387-9992

**Jizo-an Monastery** [Zen]
1603 Highland Avenue
Cinnaminson, NJ 08077
609-876-4150

**Philadelphia Buddhist
Association**
97 E. Bells Mills Road
Philadelphia, PA 19118
610-660-9269

**Tibetan Buddhist Center
of Philadelphia** [Tibetan]
3635 Lancaster Avenue
Philadelphia, PA 19104
215-222-4840

**Plum Tree Zendo** [Zen]
214 Monroe Street
Philadelphia, PA 19147
215-625-2601

**Zen Group of Reading
Aikido Makoto Dojo**
610-372-5511

## *New York*

**Village Zendo** [Zen]
Greenwich Village,
New York City
212-674-0832

**Community of
Mindfulness** [Zen]
New York City
212-501-2652

**Zen Center of New York**
212-654-1591

**Chogye International Zen
Center**
400 East 14th Street, #2E
New York, NY 10003
212-353-0461

**New York Shambhala Center** [Tibetan]
118 West 22nd Street, 6th floor
New York, NY 10011
212-675-6544

**Asian Classics Institute**
[Tibetan/Gelugpa]
PO Box 20373
New York, NY 10009
212-475-7752

**Soho Zendo**
464 West Broadway
New York, NY 10012
212-460-9289

**Palden Sakya Center**
4-10 West 101 Street, #63
New York, NY 10025-1603
212-866-4339

**Sang-ngak-cho-dzong**
[Tibetan/Nyingma]
PO Box 247, Chelsea Station
New York, NY 10113
212-439-4780

**Westchester Buddhist Meditation Group**
914-762-3231

**Empty Hand Zendo** [Zen]
624 Milton Road
Rye, NY 10580
914-921-3327

**Brooklyn Buddhist Association** [Pure Land/ Zen]
211 Smith Street
Brooklyn, NY 11201
718-488-9511

**Brooklyn Zen Urban Temple** [Soto Zen]
21 S. Elliott Place
Brooklyn, NY 11217

**Ch'an Meditation Center**
90-56 Corona Avenue
Elmhurst, NY 11373
718-592-6593

**Three Cranes Zen Center**
77 Bedford Road
Katonah, NY 10536
914-234-6658

**Dai Bosatsu Zendo** [Zen]
HRC 1 Box 171
Livingston Manor, NY 12758
914-439-4566

**Zen Mountain Monastery**
PO Box 197TR
Mt. Tremper, NY 12457
914-688-2228

**Kinpuan**—Zen Mountain
    Monastery Affiliate
Albany, NY
518-432-4676

**Karuna Tendai Dharma
    Center** [Tendai/Mixed]
PO Box 323
Canaan, NY 12029
518-392-7963

**Zen Center of Syracuse**
266 West Seneca Turnpike
Syracuse, NY 13207
315-492-9773

**Springwater Center for
    Meditative Inquiry and
    Retreats** [Mixed]
7179 Mill Street
Springwater, NY 14560
716-669-2141

**Rochester Zen Center**
7 Arnold Park
Rochester, NY 14607
716-473-9180

*Southeast*

**Insight Meditation
    Community of
    Washington**
301-891-2780

**IMC-USA** [Theravada]
438 Bankard Road
Westminster, MD 21158
410-346-7889

**Ekoji Buddhist Sangha**
[Mixed]
Richmond, VA
804-355-6657

**Stone Mountain Zendo**
[Zen]
2702 Avenel Avenue SW
Roanoke, VA 24015
703-345-8209

**Mountain Light Retreat Center** [Vipassana]
Route 2, Box 419
Crozet, VA 22432
804-478-7770

**Spencer Buddhist Meditation Group**
Route 2, Box 99
Harmony, WV 25243
304-927-1505

**Bhavana Society**
[Theravada]
Route 1 Box 218-3
High View, WV 26808
304-856-3241

**Kadampa Center** [Tibetan]
7404-G Chapel Hill Road
Raleigh, NC 27607
919-859-3433

**Shambhala Center/ Dharmadhatu** [Tibetan]
353 West Main Street
Durham, NC 27701
919-933-9082

**Durham Insight Meditation Center**
[Vipassana]
1214 Broad Street, #2
Durham, NC 27705
919-286-4754

**Charlotte Zen Meditation Society** [Soto Zen]
PO Box 32512
Charlotte, NC 28232
704-523-7373

**Southern Dharma Retreat Center** [Mixed]
Route 1, Box 34H
Hot Springs, NC 28743
704-622-7112

**Losel Shedrup Ling of Knoxville** [Tibetan]
Box 31123
Knoxville, TN 37930-1123
423-671-0472

**Delta Insight Group**
[Vipassana]
715 North Auburndale
Memphis, TN 38107
901-278-0961

**Losel Shedrup Ling Atlanta**
770-908-3358

**Atlanta Soto Zen Center**
404-659-4749

**Cypress Tree Zen Center**
PO Box 1856
Tallahassee, FL 32302

**Zen Meditation Center of Hollywood, FL**
305-860-0850

**International Zen Institute of Florida**
3860 Crawford Avenue
Miami, FL 33133
305-448-8969

**Tampa Karma Thegsum Choling** [Tibetan Karma Kagyu]
820 MacDill Avenue
Tampa, FL 33609
813-870-2904

**Wat Buddharangsi**
[Vipassana]
Miami, FL 33032
305-245-2702

**Bodhi Tree Dhamma Center** [Theravada/ Vipassana]
11355 Dauphin Avenue
Largo, FL 34648
813-392-7698

**Green Mountain Zen Center**
508 Ward Avenue
Huntsville, AL 35801
205-882-0513

**Granthi Buddhist
Association, Inc.**
345 Ulman Avenue
Bay St. Louis, MS 39520
601-467-0213

**Meditation Sangha of
Louisville** [Mixed]
502-569-1887

**Dhongak Tharling**
[Dzogchen/Nyingma]
4518 St. Ann Street
New Orleans, LA 70119
504-488-4613

**New Orleans Zen Temple**
[Soto Zen]
748 Camp Street
New Orleans, LA 70130
504-523-1213

*Midwest*

**Columbus Karma
Thegsum Choling**
[Tibetan/Karma Kagyu]
231 South Grubb Street
Columbus, OH 43215

**Mindfulness Meditation
of Columbus** [Vipassana]
2938 Monarch Drive
Columbus, OH 43235-3209
614-761-7953

**Dharma Center of
Cincinnati** [Zen/Vipassana/
Meditative Inquiry]
PO Box 23337
Cincinnati, OH 45223
513-281-6453

**Yellow Springs Dharma
Center**
502 Livermore Street
Yellow Springs, OH 45387
513-767-9919

**Indianapolis Zen Group**
[Kwan Um]
6009 North Compton
Indianapolis, IN 46220
317-924-3856

**Ganden Dheling Buddhist
Temple** [Tibetan/Gelugpa]
PO Box 2242
Bloomington, IN 47402-2242
812-337-6114

**Jewel Heart Dharma
Center** [Tibetan]
PO Box 7933
Ann Arbor, MI 48107
313-994-3387

**Zen Buddhist Temple-
Ann Arbor** [Korean Zen]
1214 Packard Road
Ann Arbor, MI 48104
313-761-6520

**Deep Spring Center**
[Vipassana]
3455 Charing Cross Road
Ann Arbor, MI 48108
313-971-3455

**Detroit Zen Center**
11464 Mitchell Street
Hamtramck, MI 48212
313-366-7738

**Tekchen Choling** [Tibetan/
Gelugpa]
60933 N. Main Street
Jones, MI 49061-9704
616-244-5474

**Iowa City Zen Center**
226 South Johnson Street,
Apt. 2A
Iowa City, IA 52240
319-338-5748

**Unitarian Church North
Zen Group**
Mequon, WI 53092
414-961-2103

**Milwaukee Zen Center**
[Soto Zen]
2825 N. Stowell Avenue
Milwaukee, WI 53211
414-963-0526

**Madison Zen Center**
1820 Jefferson Street
Madison, WI 53711
608-255-4488

**Minnesota Zen Meditation Center**
3343 East Calhoun Parkway
Minneapolis, MN 55408
612-822-5313

**Clouds in Water Meditation** [Zen]
Minneapolis, MN
612-798-5821

**Chicago Zen Center**
2029 Ridge Avenue
Evanston, IL 60201
847-475-3015

**Udumbara Zen Center Central** [Soto Zen]
Evanston, IL
847-475-3264

**Nichirin Temple of Chicago**
773-348-2028

**Zen Buddhist Temple**
[Korean Zen]
1710 West Cornelia
Chicago, IL 60657
312-528-8685

**Dharmadhatu/Shambhala Chicago** [Tibetan]
3340 North Clark Street
Chicago, IL 60657
312-472-7776

**Missouri Zen Center**
220 Spring
Webster Groves (St. Louis), MO 63119
314-961-6138

**Kansas City Zen Group**
816-471-8052

**Mid America Dharma Group** [Theravada]
Kansas City area
913-685-3430

**Mindfulness Meditation
Foundation** [American
Buddhist]
3077 Merriam Lane
Kansas City, KS 66106
913-432-7787

**Wichita Buddhist
Meditation Group**
1818 Clayton
Wichita, KS 67203
316-945-5781

**Kearney Zendo** [Zen]
3715 Avenue F
Kearney, NE 68847
308-236-5650

**Zen Center of Hot
Springs**
PO Box 1260
Hot Springs, AR 71902-1260
501-767-6096

*West*

**Vajradakini Buddhist
Center** [Kadampa]
4915 Junius Street
Dallas, TX 75214
214-823-6386

**Maria Kannon Zen Center**
7422 Vilianova Street
Dallas, TX 75225
214-361-1066

**Houston Zen Community**
PO Box 54229
Houston, TX 77254-2299
713-880-1030

**Rigpe Dorje Center**
[Tibetan]
PO Box 690995
San Antonio, TX 78230
210-525-8625

**Insight Meditation Dallas**
[Vipassana]
PO Box 781632
Dallas, TX 75378
214-351-3789

**One Zendo** [Soto Zen/Gay,
Bisexual]
PO Box 644
Santa Fe, NM 87504

**Denver Zen Center**
1233 Columbine Street #T2
Denver, CO 80206
303-333-4844

**Great Mountain Zen
Center**
Boulder, CO
303-939-9670

**Tara Mandala** [Tibetan]
PO Box 3040
Pagosa Springs, CO 81147
970-264-6177

**Kanzeon Zen Center**
1274 E. South Temple
Salt Lake City, UT 84102
801-328-8414

**Beginner's Mind Zendo**
Chandler, AZ 85223
602-963-8766

**Jodo Shu Dharma Center**
[Pure Land]
229 E. Palo Verde Street
Gilbert, AZ 85296
602-545-7684

**Hidden Mountain Zen
Center**
216 Ninth Street NW
Albuquerque, NM 87102
505-248-0649

**Taos Vipassana Sangha**
HCR 74, Box 22251,
El Prado, NM 87529
505-751-2132

**Kagyu Shempen Kunchab**
[Tibetan/Karma Kagyu]
751 Airport Road
Santa Fe, NM 87505
505-471-1152

**Ocamora Foundation**
PO Box 43
Ocate, NM 87734
505-666-2389

**Zen Community of Oregon**
PO Box 310
Corbett, OR 97019
503-282-7879

**Dharma Rain Zen Center**
[Soto Zen]
1539 SE Madison
Portland, OR 97214
503-239-4846

**Portland Shambhala Center** [Tibetan]
1110 SE Alder Street, Suite 204
Portland, OR 97214
503-231-4971

**Laughing Frog Sangha**
[Zen & Vipassana]
PO Box 1447
Poulsbo, WA 98370
360-598-4247

**Friends of the Western Buddhist Order**
2455 George Washington Way
Richland, WA 99352
509-967-2331

**Zen Center of Hawaii**
PO Box 2066
Kamuela, HI 96743

**Honolulu Diamond Sangha** [Zen]
Palolo Zen Center
2747 Walamao Road
Honolulu, HI 96816
808-735-1347

**Nichirin Mission of Hawaii**
33 Pulelehua Way
Honolulu, HI 96817
808-595-3517

**Anchorage Zen Community** [Soto Zen]
2401 Susitna
Anchorage, AK 99517
907-248-1049

## *California*

**Zen Center of Los Angeles**
923 South Normandie Avenue
Los Angeles, CA 90006-1301
213-387-2351

**Lesbian Zen Group**
[Vietnamese Zen]
928 South New Hampshire
Avenue
Los Angeles, CA 90006
213-738-9952

**International Buddhist**
**Meditation Center**
[Vietnamese Zen]
924 S. New Hampshire
Avenue
Los Angeles, CA 90006

**Dhamma Dena** [Vipassana]
65620 Giant Rock
Joshua Tree, CA
619-362-4815

**Manzanita Village Retreat**
**Center** [Mixed]
Southern California
619-782-3604

**Desert Zen Center**
10989 Buena Vista
Lucerne Valley, CA 92356
619-248-7404

**Karma Mahasiddha Ling**
[Tibetan]
PO Box 1441
Idyllwild, CA 92549
909-659-3401

**Zen Mountain Center**
PO Box 43
Mountain Center, CA 92561
909-659-5272

**Newport Mesa Zen Center**
711 West 17th Street A8
Costa Mesa, CA 92627
714-631-5389

**Shingon Buddhist**
**International Institute**
[Koyasan Shingon]
PO Box 3757
Fresno, CA 93650-3757

**Tse Chen Ling Center for Tibetan Buddhist Studies**
4 Joost Avenue
San Francisco, CA 94131
415-339-8002

**Gay Buddhist Fellowship**
2261 Market Street #422
San Francisco, CA 94114
415-974-9878

**San Francisco Zen Center**
415-863-3136
(San Francisco)
415-383-3134
(Sausalito)

**Sang-ngak-cho-dzong**
[Tibetan/Nyingma]
2508 Eagle Avenue
Alameda, CA 94501
510-865-1394

**San Francisco Saraha Buddist Center**
[Kadampa]
415-585-9161

**Spirit Rock Meditation Center** [Vipassana]
PO Box 909
Woodacre, CA 94973
415-488-0164

**Vajrapani Institute**
[Tibetan]
PO Box 2130
Boulder Creek, CA 95006
408-338-6654

**Shasta Abbey** [Soto Zen]
PO Box 199
Mt. Shasta, CA 96067
916-926-4208

**Nichirin Order of North America**
3570 Mona Way
San Jose, CA 95130
408-246-0111

**Sonoma Mountain Zen Center**
6367 Sonoma Mountain Road
Santa Rosa, CA 95404
707-545-8105

**Stone Creek Zendo** [Soto
 Zen]
PO Box 1053
Sebastopol, CA 95473
707-829-9808

**Lion's Roar Mandala**
 [Integral Dharma]
3550 Watt Avenue, Suite 2
Sacramento, CA 95821
916-481-0424

## International

**Zen Fellowship**
PO Box 273
Powell River, BC, Canada
 V8A 4Z6

**Zen Buddhist Temple**
 [Korean Zen]
86 Vaughan Road
Toronto, ON, Canada
 M6C 2M1
416-658-0137

**Centre Zen de la Main**
30 rue Vallieres
Montreal, QC Canada
 H2W 1C2
514-842-3648

# Contributors

STEPHEN BATCHELOR was born in Scotland and educated in England and in Buddhist monasteries in India, Korea, and Switzerland. He is director of studies at Sharpham College for Buddhist Studies and Contemporary Enquiry in Devon, England. A noted scholar and translator, he has written numerous books, including *The Awakening of the West* (Parallax, 1994), a classic translation of *A Guide to the Bodhisattva's Way of Life* (Library of Tibetan Works and Archives, 1979), and *Buddhism Without Beliefs* (Riverhead, 1997).

CHARLOTTE JOKO BECK, American Zen teacher, studied at the Los Angeles Zen Center with Maezumi Roshi (and was later designated his third dharma heir), Yasutani Roshi, and Soen Roshi. In 1983 she moved to the Zen Center of San Diego, where she lives and teaches. Her books on practice include *Everyday Zen* (HarperCollins, 1989) and *Nothing Special: Living Zen* (HarperCollins, 1993).

SYLVIA BOORSTEIN is a Vipassana teacher and retreat leader across the United States. She is a cofounding teacher, with Jack Kornfield, at the Spirit Rock Meditation Center in California, and is a senior teacher at the Insight Meditation Society in Massachusetts. She is the author of *Don't Just Do Something, Sit There* (HarperCollins, 1996) and *It's Easier Than You Think* (HarperCollins, 1995).

THE FOURTEENTH DALAI LAMA, TENZIN GYATSO, is considered a living embodiment of the spiritual ideal in Tibetan Buddhism. After the Chinese invasion of Tibet in 1959, he fled to India, where he established a government in exile in Dharamsala. Since then he has traveled worldwide, teaching and conducting rituals, and his contributions to world peace were recognized in 1989 when he was awarded the Nobel Peace Prize. His many writings include *A Flash of Lightning in the Dark of Night* (Shambhala, 1994) and *A Policy of Kindness* (Snow Lion, 1990).

ZEN MASTER DOGEN, a thirteenth-century Japanese aristocrat, experienced enlightenment in 1223 on a visit to China. Four years later, he returned to his homeland and founded the Japanese school of Soto Zen Buddhism. He is revered as the most important Japanese Zen master, and his writings are widely anthologized; a collection known as *Treasury of the Eye of the True Dharma* is the most well known.

JOSEPH GOLDSTEIN has studied Buddhism in India, Thailand, and Burma. In 1976 he cofounded, with Sharon Salzberg and Jack Kornfield, the Insight Meditation Society in Barre, Massachusetts. He has led meditation retreats and taught around the world for more than twenty years. Among his widely read books are *Insight Meditation* (Shambhala, 1993), *The Experience of Insight* (Shambhala, 1987), and, with Jack Kornfield, *Seeking the Heart of Wisdom* (Shambhala, 1987).

VENERABLE HENEPOLA GUNARATANA was ordained as a Buddhist monk in Sri Lanka when he was twelve years old. After missionary work in India and Malaysia and teaching in Malaysia, he came to the United States in 1968. He was president of the Buddhist Vihara Society of Washington, D.C.; and he taught at the American University, Georgetown University, and the University of Maryland. His writings on Theravadan tradition have been published in Malaysia, India, Sri Lanka, and the United States, where his book *Mindfulness in Plain English* (Wisdom Publications, 1991) is widely recognized as an extraordinarily valuable introduction to insight meditation.

JOAN HALIFAX is a Buddhist teacher in the Zen tradition and an ecologist. She is the author of *The Fruitful Darkness: Reconnecting with the Body of the Earth* (HarperCollins, 1994).

THICH NHAT HANH, a Vietnamese Zen Buddhist monk, founded the Van Hanh Buddhist University in Saigon and has taught at Columbia University in New York City and at the Sorbonne in Paris. In 1967, he was nominated by Martin Luther King, Jr. for the Nobel Peace Prize. He is the author of more than seventy-five books, including a biography of the Buddha—*Old Path / White Clouds* (Parallax, 1991)—*Present Moment, Wonderful Moment* (Parallax, 1990), *Breathe! You Are Alive* (Parallax, 1988), *Zen Keys*

(Doubleday, 1974), and *Living Buddha, Living Christ* (Riverhead 1995).

YOSHINORE HIUGA SENSEI is abbot of Kyoto Shudo-in, in Ohara, Japan. His talk "Existence and Unity" (1994) was translated by Sarah Fremerman.

LEX HIXON, as a scholar, was involved in many religious traditions and as the host of a radio program interviewed spiritual teachers. He is the author of *Living Buddha Zen* (Larson, 1995) and *The Mother of All Buddhas* (Quest Books, 1993).

JON KABAT-ZINN is associate professor of medicine and the founder and director of the Stress Reduction Clinic at the University of Massachusetts Medical Center. His clear and accessible teachings on Buddhist mindfulness in daily life have made his writings popular among a remarkably wide audience of Buddhists and non-Buddhists. His books include *Wherever You Go, There You Are* (Hyperion, 1994) and *Full Catastrophe Living* (Delta, 1991).

DAININ KATAGIRI trained at Soto Zen monasteries in Japan before moving to the United States in 1963. After residing at several monasteries in California, including the San Francisco Zen Center, where he assisted Shunryu Suzuki, he became the first abbot of the Minnesota Zen Center, in Minneapolis. *Returning to Silence* (Shambhala, 1988) is a collection of his teachings on meditation.

AYYA KHEMA, who was born in Germany and emigrated to the United States at the end of World War II, was ordained as a Buddhist nun in Sri Lanka in 1979. She has been active worldwide in supporting women Buddhists: She set up the International Buddhist Women's Centre in Sri Lanka; coordinated the first international conference of Buddhist nuns; and established Sakyadhita, a worldwide Buddhist women's organization. In 1987, she was the first Buddhist ever to address the United Nations. Her numerous books include *When the Iron Eagle Flies* (Arkana, 1991) and *Being Nobody, Going Nowhere* (Wisdom Publications, 1988).

JACK KORNFIELD was trained as a Buddhist monk in Thailand, Burma, and India. When he returned to the United States, he cofounded the Insight Meditation Society in Massachusetts and the Spirit Rock Meditation Center in California. He is recognized worldwide as an exceptional Vipassana teacher. His books include *A Path with Heart* (Bantam, 1993) and, with Joseph Goldstein, *Seeking the Heart of Wisdom* (Shambhala, 1987).

MAHASI SAYADAW is a widely respected Theravadan teacher who was born and educated in Burma. He was invited by the prime minister, after Burma achieved independence, to open a large center in Rangoon; his disciples have since opened more than one hundred meditation centers in Burma, Thailand, and Ceylon. His commentary on basic practice is included in Jack Kornfield, ed., *Living Dharma* (Shambhala, 1996).

ZEN MASTER MAN-AN was an adept of the Soto Zen school of Japanese Buddhism who is believed to have lived in the early seventeenth century. His meditation manual *An Elementary Talk on Zen* is included in Thomas Cleary, translator, *Minding Mind* (Shambhala, 1995).

KATHLEEN MCDONALD (SANGYE KHADRO) was ordained as a Tibetan Buddhist nun in 1974 and is a teacher in the Foundation for the Preservation of the Mahayana Tradition, a worldwide organization of Buddhist teaching and meditation centers. Her guide *How to Meditate* (Wisdom Publications, 1984) covers practical aspects of her teachings on meditation.

SOEN NAKAGAWA, a Zen master, is coauthor of *Namu Dai Bosa* (The Zen Studies Society)

NICHIRIN DAISHONIN founded the Nichirin school of Japanese Buddhism in the thirteenth century. His writings have appeared in English as *The Major Writings of Nichirin Daishonin* (Shoshu International Center).

PATRUL RINPOCHE is the author of *The Heart Treasure of the Enlightened Ones.*

SHARON SALZBERG, cofounder with Joseph Goldstein and Jack Kornfield of the Insight Meditation Society in Massachusetts, has taught meditation at Buddhist centers around the world. She is the author of the widely acclaimed book *Lovingkindness* (Shambhala, 1995).

JOHN SNELLING was born in Wales and educated in England. A noted scholar and author, he was general secretary of the Buddhist Society, then editor of its widely read journal, *The Middle Way*, from 1980 to 1987. His numerous writings include the book *The Elements of Buddhism* (Elements Books, 1990).

GARY SNYDER, Pulitzer Prize—winning poet and essayist, has long practiced in the Zen tradition. He is the author of *Practice of the Wild* (North Point Press, 1990).

SOGYAL RINPOCHE was born in Tibet, where he lived until 1959, when he went into exile with his master after the Chinese invasion. He was educated in Delhi and Cambridge universities and began teaching in the West in 1974. He is the founder of Rigpa Fellowship and Buddhist centers worldwide, and the author of *Meditation* (HarperCollins, 1994) and *The Tibetan Book of Living and Dying* (HarperCollins, 1992).

SHUNRYU SUZUKI was a spiritual descendant of the thirteenth-century Zen master Dogen. He came to the United States from Japan in 1958 and founded three centers, including Zen Mountain Center, the first Zen training center outside Asia. He is respected as one of the most important Zen teachers of his time, and his core teachings are recorded in *Zen Mind, Beginner's Mind* (Weath erhill, 1970).

THYNN THYNN is a Burmese medical doctor who is also an artist and dharma teacher. She has been published widely in Burma and Thailand, and her book *Living Meditation, Living Insight* (Dhamma Dana Publications, 1995) reflects traditional Theravadan teachings, expressed for laypeople.

KOSHO UCHIYAMA was born in Tokyo and educated in Western philosophy before becoming a Soto Zen priest in 1940. He became abbot of the Antaiji, a temple and monastery near Kyoto, in 1965. He wrote more than twenty texts on Zen, including translations of Dogen's works into modern Japanese. Among his writings available in English are *Opening the Hand of Thought* (Arkana, 1993) and *Refining Your Life* (Weatherhill, 1983).

B. ALAN WALLACE, one of the first Westerners ordained in the Tibetan Buddhist tradition, is a noted scholar, teacher, and translator. He has written several books stressing the relevance of Tibetan Buddhist teaching to contemporary life, including *Tibetan Buddhism from the Ground Up* (Wisdom Publications, 1993).

HAKUIN YASUTANI ROSHI is a Japanese Zen master on *kinhin*, the formal walking meditation practice in Zen monasteries. His description of the practice is excerpted from Philip Kapleau, ed., *The Three Pillars of Zen* (Doubleday, 1980).

# Credits

## PART I: WHAT IS MEDITATION?

Sogyal Rinpoche: Bringing the Mind Home. Reprinted from *The Tibetan Book of Living and Dying* by Sogyal Rinpoche. Copyright © 1993 by Rigpa Fellowship. Reprinted by permission of HarperCollins Publishers, Inc.

The Buddha: *The Greater Discourse on the Foundations of Mindfulness.* © Maurice Walshe 1987, 1995. Reprinted from *The Long Discourses of Buddha: A Translation of the Digha Nikaya* with permission of Wisdom Publications, 199 Elm Street, Somerville, Massachusetts 02144, USA.

Thich Nhat Hanh: The Four Foundations of Mindfulness. Reprinted from *Old Path White Clouds: Walking in the Footsteps of the Buddha* (1991) by Thich Nhat Hanh with permission of Parallax Press, Berkeley, California.

## PART II: WHY MEDITATE?

a division of Bantam Doubleday Dell Publishing Group, Inc.

Jon Kabat-Zinn: To Pursue Your Vision. Reprinted from *Wherever You Go, There You Are: Mindfulness Meditation in Everyday Life* by Jon Kabat-Zinn. Copyright © 1994 Jon Kabat-Zinn. Reprinted with permission by Hyperion.

Shunryu Suzuki: For Enlightenment. Reprinted from *Zen Mind, Beginner's Mind* by Shunryu Suzuki. Copyright © 1970 by Shunryu Suzuki. Reprinted by permission of Weatherhill, Inc.

## PART III: HOW TO MEDITATE

The Buddha: *The Greater Discourse on the Foundations of Mindfulness.* © Bhikkhu Bodhi 1995. Reprinted from *The Middle Length Discourse of the Buddha: A New Translation of the Majjhima Nikaya* with permission of Wisdom Publications, 199 Elm Street, Somerville, Massachusetts 02144, USA.

Jack Kornfield: Establishing a Daily Meditation Practice. From *A Path with Heart* by Jack Kornfield. Copyright © 1993 by Jack Kornfield. Used by permission of Bantam Books, a division of Bantam Doubleday Dell Publishing Group, Inc.

Zen Master Dogen: Zen Meditation Instructions. From *Minding Mind: A Course in Basic Meditation,* translated by Thomas Cleary, © 1995. Reprinted by arrangement with Shambhala Publications, Inc., 300 Massachusetts Avenue, Boston, MA 02115.

The Dalai Lama: Tibetan Meditation Instructions. *The Dalai Lama: A Policy of Kindness,* compiled and edited Sidney Piburn.

## Posture

Shunryu Suzuki: The Oneness of Duality. Reprinted from *Zen Mind, Beginner's Mind* by Shunryu Suzuki, 1970. Used by permission of Weatherhill, Inc.

Jon Kabat-Zinn: Dignity. Reprinted from *Wherever You Go, There You Are: Mindfulness Meditation in Everyday Life* by Jon Kabat-Zinn. Copyright © 1994 Jon Kabat-Zinn. Reprinted with permission by Hyperion.

## Breathing

The Buddha: *Sutra on the Full Awareness of Breathing*. Reprinted from *Breathe! You Are Alive: Sutra on the Full Awareness of Breathing* (1996) by Thich Nhat Hanh with permission of Parallax Press, Berkeley, California.

Zen Master Man-an: Tuning the Breathing. From *Minding Mind: A Course in Basic Meditation,* translated by Thomas Cleary, © 1995. Reprinted by arrangement with Shambhala Publications, Inc., 300 Massachusetts Ave., Boston, MA 02115.

Venerable Henepola Gunaratana: Taming a Wild Elephant. © Henepola Gunaratana 1991. Reprinted from *Mindfulness in Plain English* with permission of Wisdom Publications, 199 Elm Street, Somerville, Massachusetts 02144, USA.

Shunryu Suzuki: The Swinging Door. Reprinted from *Zen Mind, Beginner's Mind* by Shunryu Suzuki, 1970. Used by permission of Weatherhill, Inc.

Ayya Khema: Ways of Using the Breath. From *When the Iron Eagle Flies*, 1991. Copyright © Ayya Khema, 1991. Penguin Books, 27 Wrights Lane, London W8 5TZ.

Mahasi Sayadaw: Exercise/Breathing From *Living Dharma* by Jack Kornfield, © 1977, 1996. Reprinted by arrangement with

## Walking

The Buddha: *The Greater Discourse on the Foundations of Mindfulness.* © Maurice Walshe 1987, 1995. Reprinted from *The Long Discourses of Buddha: A Translation of the Digha Nikaya* with permission of Wisdom Publications, 199 Elm Street, Somerville, Massachusetts 02144, USA.

Hakuin Yasutani Roshi: Kinhin. From *The Three Pillars of Zen* by Philip Kapleau. Copyright © 1965, 1989 by Philip Kapleau. Copyright © 1980 by The Zen Center, Inc. Used by permission of Doubleday, a division of Bantam Doubleday Dell Publishing Group, Inc.

Joan Halifax: The Mind of Practice Embodied. Reprinted by permission from *Tricycle* magazine, Summer 1996, Volume 5, No. 4.

Sylvia Boorstein: Exercise/Walking. Reprinted from *Don't Just Sit There, Do Something* by Sylvia Boorstein. Copyright © 1996 by Sylvia Boorstein. Reprinted by permission of HarperCollins Publishers, Inc.

## Driving

Thich Nhat Hanh: Driving Meditation. Reprinted from *Present Moment Wonderful Moment: Mindfulness Verse for Daily Living* (1990) by Thich Nhat Hanh with permission of Parallax Press, Berkeley, California.

## Eating

Thich Nhat Hanh: Eating a Tangerine. Reprinted from *Old Path White Clouds: Walking in the Footsteps of the Buddha* (1991) by Thich Nhat Hanh with permission of Parallax Press, Berkeley, California.

Joseph Goldstein: Exercise/Breathing. From *The Experience of Insight* by Joseph Goldstein, © 1987. Reprinted by arrangement with Shambhala Publications, Inc., 300 Massachusetts Avenue, Boston, MA 02115.

## Using Mantras

Lex Hixon: *The Heart Sutra*. Reprinted from *Tricycle: The Buddhist Review*, volume IV, number 4.

Patrul Rinpoche: *Mani*. From *The Heart Treasure of the Enlightened Ones* by Dilgo Khyentse, © 1992. Reprinted by arrangement with Shambhala Publications, Inc., 300 Massachusetts Avenue, Boston, MA 02115.

Nichiren Daishonin: *The Lotus Sutra*. Reprinted from *The Major Writings of Nichiren Daishonin*, volume one, translated and published by NSIC, Tokyo, 1979.

Yoshinori Hiuga Sensei: Existence and Unity. From a speech given by Abbot Yoshinori Hiuga Sensei at Kyoto Monastery, Kyoto Shudo-in in Ohara, Japan. Reprinted by permission of Kyoto Kitayama Shudo-in.

Soen Nakagawa: Everything Condensed. Reprinted from *Namu Dai Bosa: A Transmission of Zen Buddhism in America* by N.

## Listening

## Visualization

## Feelings and Metta

## Problems in Meditating

## POSTSCRIPT

# Index

Abdomen, focus on, 163–65
Abhisheka (initiation rites), 35
Advertising your meditation, 241
Aggregates (skandhas), 15
Aimlessness (apranahita), 170
Air, 67
Altar for meditation, 108
American Indian style of sitting, 129
Amitabha Buddha, 32
Analytical meditation, 200
Ananda, Venerable, 13
"Anapanasati Sutta" (Buddha), 144–50
Anatman (nonself), 31
Anchorage Zen Community (Soto Zen), 256
Anitya (impermanence), 31
Apranahita (aimlessness), 170
Archetypal patterns, 36
Arms, 134, 140
"Art of Awakening, The" (Kornfield), 17–25
Asian Classics Institute (Tibetan/Gelugpa), 256
Atman (self), 31
Attention, level of, 18
"Attention to Emotions," Thynn Thynn, 205–7
Attentiveness practice, 173
Attitude for meditation, 24
Automatic reactions, 29
Avalokiteshvara (diety), 199

Awakening, 17–25, 71
  Seven Factors of, 16
Awareness
  of Earth, 170–72
  and meditation, 29–30
"Awareness, no blame, change," 160

Back, 127, 135
Balance, 127
Balancing what is reactive, 74–76
Barre Center for Buddhist Studies (mixed traditions), 244
Barrington Zen Center, 244
Batchelor, Stephen, 261
  "Going Against the Stream," 26–28
Beck, Charlotte Joko, 261
  "What Practice Is," 53–56
  "What Practice Is Not," 50–52
Beginner's Mind Zendo, 255
Bhavana (mind training), 83
Bhavana Society (Theravada), 249
Bija (seed mantra), 36, 186
Blissful states, 50
Blue Cliff Record, 34
Bodhi Tree Dhamma Center (Theravada/ Vipassana), 250
Bodhidharma, 37, 103

Bodhisattvic (enlightened being), 31, 41
Body
  energy flow in, 73
  as a foundation of mindfulness, 11, 14
  healing of, 94–96
  in meditation, 126–32
  and mind, 138
  as skandha, 15
  tensions in, 109
  See also Postures
Body of light meditation exercise, 203–4
Boorstein, Sylvia, 262
  "Exercise/Sound Meditation," 196–97
  "Exercise/Walking," 173–76
Boston Jodo Mission (Pure Land), 244
Breathing, 144–65
  counting, 34, 231–38
  exercise for, 163–65
  impermanence of, 161–62
  as non-conceptual process, 154
  noticing, 116–17
  as a present-time process, 155
  sensations of, 109–10
Breathing meditation, 20–21, 34
"Bringing the Mind Home" (Sogyal Rinpoche), 5–
  10
Brooklyn Buddhist Association (Pure Land/Zen),
  247
Booklyn Zen Urban Temple [Soto Zen], 247
Buddha
  Amitabha, 32
  Gautama, 5–7
  "Greater Discourse of Advice to Rahula, The,"
    66–68
  "Greater Discourse on the Foundations of
    Mindfulness, The," 11–12, 65, 107, 166–67
  historical, 5–7
  "Maha-Assapura Sutta," 219–21
  "Sutra on the Full Awareness of Breathing,"
    144–50
  teaching children, 180–82
Buddha-dharma (Buddha-law), 33
Buddhist meditation and study centers, 243–259
"Buddhist Traditions of Meditation" (Snelling), 29–
  36
Burmese style of sitting, 129

Calm abiding (shamatha), 30–31. See also Samatha
Cambridge Insight Meditation Center (Vipassana),
  244
Cambridge Zen Center, 244
Camus, Albert, The Stranger, 70

Center for the Awareness of Pattern (Soto Zen),
  244
Center for Dzogchen Studies (Nyingma/Kagyu),
  New Haven, CT, 246
Centre Zen del la Main, 259
Chairs, 128, 131
Ch'an Meditation Center, 247
Ch'an (Zen meditation in China), 33
Chanting, 19
Charlotte Zen Meditation Society (Soto Zen), 249
Chenrezi, Bodhisattva of Compassion, 188–89
Chicago Zen Center, 253
Children, Buddha teaching, 180–82
China
  and Pure Land meditation, 32
  and Zen meditation, 33
Chögyam Trungpa, 262
Chogye International Zen Center, 246
Christian Desert Fathers, 24
Clothing for meditation, 111, 128–29
Clouds in Water Meditation (Zen), 253
Columbus Karma Thegsum Choling (Tibetan/
  Karma Kagyu), 251
Community, support in, 123–25
Community of Mindfulness (Zen), 246
Community (sangha), 123–25
Concentration, 69, 70
  developing, 30–31, 231
  level of, 18, 20, 22–24
  versus meditation, 44–46
"Concentration and Meditation" (Thynn Thynn),
  44–46
Concepts and reality exercise, 80–81
Consciousness
  on breathing, 151, 231
  everyday survival, 82–83
  sense and mental, 114
  as skandha, 15
  transcendental, 82–87
  transformation of, 209
Control, need for, 157
Cosmic mudra, 140
"Counting Breaths" (Yasutani Roshi), 231–32
Counting practice, 34, 231–38
Culture and meditation, 100
Cushions, 128, 129
Cypress Tree Zen Center, 250

Dai Bosatsu Zendo, 248
Daily experience, 205
Daily meditation practice, 108–10
"Daimoku" (mantra), 191

Dalai Lama (14th), 262
  "Tibetan Meditation Instructions," 112–15
Danger, freedom from, 212
Deep Spring Center (Vipassana), 252
Deities, meditating on, 199, 202
Delta Insight Group (Vipassana), 250
Denver Zen Center, 255
Desert Zen Center, 257
Detroit Zen Center, 252
Dhamma Dena (Vipassana), 257
*Dhammapada, The,* "The Mind," 88–89
Dharanis (mantras), 186
Dharma Center of Cincinnati (Zen/Vipassana/
  Meditative Inquiry), 251
Dharma pain, 74
Dharma Rain Zen Center (Soto Zen), 256
Dharmadhatu/Shambhala Chicago (Tibetan), 253
Dharmas (phenomena), 16, 42
Dhongak Tharling (Dzogchen/Nyingma), 251
"Die on purpose," 48
Diety (avalokiteshvara), 199
"Dignity" (Kabat-Zinn), 142–43
Direct experience, 76–78, 80–81
Discourse (sutra), 13
Dissatisfaction, 97
Distractions
  and focus, 153
  and ignorance, 6
  and meditation, 21, 117, 197, 216
  and visualization, 201
Distress, 65
Dogen (Japanese Zen master), 33, 34, 37–39, 262
  "Zen Meditation Instructions," 111–12
Doubt, 15, 220, 222–30
Dream, waking, 29
"Driving Meditation" (Hanh), 177–79
Drowsiness, 15, 128
Duality, 40–41, 97
  oneness of, 138–41
  and universal existence, 159
Dudjom Rinpoche, 218
Duhkha (suffering), 31
Dukkha (unsatisfactoriness), 84
Durham Insight Meditation Center (Vipassana),
  249

Earth, 66
  awareness of, 170–72
Ease of well-being, 213
Eating exercise, 183–85
Eating meditation, 180–85
"Eating a Tangerine" (Hanh), 180–82

Ekoji Buddhist Sangha (mixed), 249
Emptiness (shunyata), 31, 35
Empty Hand Zendo, 247
Enlightened being (bodhisattvic), 31, 41
Enlightenment, 5, 6, 37, 69, 103–4
"Establishing a Daily Meditation Practice"
  (Kornfield), 108–10
Ethical discipline, 90–91
"Everything Condensed" (Nakagawa), 194–95
Evil and good, 40
"Exercise/Body of Light Meditation" (McDonald),
  203–4
"Exercise/Breathing," (Mahasi Sayadaw), 163–65
"Exercise/Concepts and Reality" (Goldstein), 80–
  81
"Exercise/Eating" (Goldstein), 183–85
"Exercise/Hindrances" (Kornfield), 239–40
"Exercise/Lovingkindness" (Salzberg), 214–15
"Exercise/Stopping" (Kabat-Zinn), 49
"Exercise/Walking (Boorstein), 173–76
"Existence and Unity" (Hiuga Sensei), 192–93
Experience, direct, 76–78, 80–81
Exploring what is hidden, 76–79
External conditions for meditation, 21–22
Eyes, 130, 165
  closed, 109, 135, 197
  open, 112, 113–14

Feelings
  as a foundation of mindfulness, 11, 14–15
  healing of, 96
  and metta, 205–15
  as skandha, 15
Fire, 67
"Five Houses," T'ang dynasty (China), 33
Food. *See* Eating meditation
"For Enlightenment" (Suzuki), 103–4
Forgetfulness, 70
Four foundations of mindfulness, 65, 144, 147–48,
  166
"Four Foundations of Mindfulness" (Hanh), 13–
  16
Four Noble Truths, 16
Freedom from danger, 212
Friends of the Western Buddhist Order, 256
Full-lotus posture, 111, 130, 134, 138
Future, 155, 162
FWBO Aryloka Retreat Center, 245

Ganden Dheling Buddhist Temple (Tibetan/
  Gelugpa), 252
Gassho (greeting of respect), 42

"Gate gate paragate parasamgate bodhi svaha"
    (mantra), 187
Gateless Gate, 34
Gathas (brief verses), 177
Gautama Buddha, 5–7
Gay Buddhist Fellowship, 258
"Going Against the Stream" (Batchelor), 26–28
Goldstein, Joseph, 262
    "Exercise/Concepts and Reality," 80–81
    "Exercise/Eating," 183–85
    "Hindrances," 222–30
    "To Open, To Balance, To Explore," 72–79
    "Training of the Heart," 208–10
    "Vipassana Meditation Instructions," 116–20
Good and evil, 40
Granthi Buddhist Association, Inc., 251
"Great Teacher, The," (Gunaratana), 60–62
"Greater Discourse of Advice to Rahula, The"
    (Buddha), 66–68
"Greater Discourse on the Foundations of
    Mindfulness, The" (Buddha), 11–12, 65,
    107, 166–67
Great Mountain Zen Center, 255
Greed, 223
Green Mountain Zen Center, 250
Grief, healing of, 96
Group meditation, 22, 123–25, 157
Gunaratana, Venerable Henepola, 263
    "Great Teacher, The," 60–62
    "Taming a Wild Elephant," 153–57
    "What to Do with Your Body," 126–32
    "When the Mind Wanders," 233–38

Half-lotus posture, 111, 130, 134
Halifax, Joan, 263
    "Mind of Practice Embodied, The," 170–72
Hands, 113, 130, 134, 140
Hanh, Thich Nhat, 144, 263
    on the Buddha's enlightenment, 6
    "Driving Meditation," 177–79
    "Eating a Tangerine," 180–82
    "Four Foundations of Mindfulness," 13–16
    "To Achieve Necessary Awareness," 69–71
Happiness, 212, 213
Hatha yoga, 136–37
Hatred, 219, 222–30
Head, 127, 136
Healing, 94–99
Health, 213
Health benefits, 51–52
Heart, healing of, 96
"Heart center," 208–10

Heart and mind, 208–9
"Heart Sutra, The" (Hixon), 186–87
Here-and-now, 156, 157, 205–6. See also Present
    moment
Hidden Mountain Zen Center, 255
Higher understanding (panna), 44, 207
Hindrances, 219–30
Hindrances exercise, 239–40
"Hindrances" (Goldstein), 222–30
Hiuga Sensei, Yoshinore, 264
    "Existence and Unity," 192–93
Hixon, Les, 264
    "Heart Sutra, The," 186–87
Honolulu Diamond Sangha (Zen), 256
Houston Zen Community, 254
Humor, sense of, 24, 25

Ignorance, 91
    and enlightenment, 6
    and karma, 227
Ill will, 15, 219, 222–30
Illusion, 70, 193
    and reality, 154
IMC-USA (Theravada), 248
Impermanence, 31, 77–79, 196
    of breathing, 161–62
Indianapolis Zen Group (Kwan Um), 252
Initiation rites (abhisheka), 35
Inner calm (samatha), 28
Inner world and outer world, 158–59
Insight meditation, 27–28. See also Vipashyana;
    Vipassana
Insight Meditation Community of Washington,
    248
Insight Meditation Dallas [Vipassana], 255
Insight Meditation Society (Vipassana), 244
Insight-wisdom, 44–46
Inspirational reading, 22, 108
International Buddhist Meditation Center
    [Vietnamese Zen], 257
International Zen Institute of Florida, 250
Iowa City Zen Center, 252

Japan
    and Pure Land meditation, 32
    and Zen meditation, 33
Jaws, 135
Jewel Heart Dharma Center (Tibetan), 252
Jizo-an Monastery (Zen), 246
Jodo and Jodo-shin schools, 32
Joriki (personal power), 51
Joyce, James, 94

"Just One Breath" (Snyder), 57–59

Kabat-Zinn, Jon, 264
  "Dignity," 142–43
  "Exercise/Stopping," 49
  "Keeping It Simple," 241
  "Stopping and Being Present," 47–48
  "To Pursue Your Vision," 100–102
Kadampa Center (Tibetan), 249
Kagyu Shempen Kunchab (Tibetan/Karma Kagyu), 255
Kagyupa order of Tibetan Buddhism, 91
Kansas City Zen Group, 253
Kanzeon Zen Center, 255
Karma, 227
Karma Chagme, 188
Karma Mahasiddha Ling (Tibetan), 257
Karmê-Chöling Buddhist and Shambala Meditation Center (Tibetan), 245
Karuna Tendai Dharma Center (Tendai/Mixed), 248
Katagiri, Dainin, 264
  "Mindfulness as the Middle Way," 40–43
Kearney Zendo, 254
"Keeping It Simple" (Kabat-Zinn), 241
Khema, Ayya, 264
  "To Transcend Everyday Consciousness," 82–87
  "Ways of Using the Breath," 160–62
"Kinhin" (Yasutani Roshi), 168–69
Kinpuan (Zen Mountain Monastery Affiliate), 248
Koan practice, 34–35
Kornfield, Jack, 265
  "Art of Awakening, The," 17–25
  "Establishing a Daily Meditation Practice," 108–10
  "Exercise/Hindrances," 239–40
  "Sangha and Retreat," 123–25
  "To Heal the Body, Heart, and Mind," 94–99
Kung-an. See Koan practice
Kurukulla Center (Tibetan), 244

Labeling, 197
  of sensations, 109, 117–19
  of thoughts, 55–56, 87, 109, 117–19
Laughing Frog Sangha (Zen and Vipassana), 256
Legs, 133–34, 163
Lesbian Zen Group (Vietnamese Zen), 257
Liberation, hindrances to, 15
Lin-chi (Japanese Rinzai), 33
Lion's Roar Mandala [Integral Dharma], 259

Lips, 112
Listening meditation, 196–97
Living Dharma Center (Zen)
  Amherst, MA, 244
  Bolton, CT, 245
Losel Shedrup Ling Atlanta, 250
Losel Shedrup Ling of Knoxville (Tibetan), 250
"Lotus Sutra, The" (Nichirin Daishonin), 190–91
Lovingkindness exercise, 214–15
Lovingkindness (metta), 205–15

McDonald, Kathleen, 266
  "Exercise/Body of Light Meditation," 203–4
  "Seven-Point Posture," 133–37
  "Thinking in Pictures," 198–202
Madison Zen Center, 253
"Maha-Assapura Sutta" (Buddha), 219–21
"Mahasatipatthana Sutta." See "The Greater Discourse on the Foundations of Mindfulness"
Mahasi Sayadaw, 265
  "Exercise/Breathing," 163–65
Mahayana Buddhism, 31, 42
Man-an, 265
  "Tuning the Breathing," 151–52
Mandala Buddhist Center (Shingon), 245
Mandala (symbolic cosmology), 35
"Mani" (Patrul Rinpoche), 188–89
Mantras, 20, 186–95
  seed, 36, 186
Manzanita Village Retreat Center (mixed), 260
Mara (overwhelming passions), 89
Maria Kennon Zen Center, 254
Meditation
  analytical, 200
  as "Art of Awakening, 17–25
  and awareness, 29–30
  beginners in, 163–65, 231
  breathing, 20–21, 34
  Buddhist traditions of, 29–36
  and culture, 100
  daily practice, 108–10
  driving, 177–79
  eating, 180–85
  and enlightenment, 5–10, 37
  external conditions for, 21–22
  group, 22, 123–25, 157
  insight (vipassana), 27–28
  listening, 196–97
  methods of, 83
  one-breath, 57–59
  place for, 108

problems in, 216–40
simpleness of, 107
stabilizing, 200
study centers for, 243–259
talking about, 241
as The Great Teacher, 60–62
time for, 108, 115
versus concentration, 44–46
walking, 166–67
zazen, 33
Meditation Sangha of Louisville [Mixed], 251
Meditative quiescence, 91–93
Mental formations as skandha, 15
Mental happiness, 212
Mental noting, 118–19. See also Labeling
Metta (lovingkindness), 205–15
"Metta Practice" (Salzberg), 211–13
Mid America Dharma Group (Theravada), 253
Middle Way, The, 40–43
Milarepa Center (Tibetan), 245
Milwaukee Zen Center (Soto Zen), 252
Mind
   and body, 138
   chattering of, 84, 85
   as a foundation of mindfulness, 11, 15
   healing of, 97–99
   scattered, 19, 75
"Mind of Practice Embodied, The" (Halifax), 170–72
"Mind, The, Dhammapada, The, 88–89
Mind training (bhavana), 83
Mindfulness, 30, 69
   in bringing your mind home, 9
   four foundations of, 11–12, 13–16
Mindfulness Meditation of Columbus (Vipassana), 251
Mindfulness Meditation Foundation (American Buddhist), 254
"Mindfulness as the Middle Way" (Katagiri), 40–43
Mindfulness Sangha, 245
Mind-objects as a foundation of mindfulness, 11, 15–16
"Mind's Own Radiance, The" (Sogyal Rinpoche), 216–18
Minnesota Zen Meditation Center, 253
Missouri Zen Center, 253
Monasteries, 124
Morgan Bay Zendo (mixed traditions), 244
Mountain Light Retreat Center (Vipassana), 249
Mouth, 113
Muscular armor, 96
Muscular fatigue, 127

Nakagawa, Soen, 266
   "Everything Condensed," 194–95
   "Nam myoho renge kyo" (mantra), 190–91
   "Namu amida butsu" (mantra), 192–93
   "Namu dai bosa" (mantra), 194–95
   "Nembutsu" (mantra), 192–93
New Haven Shambhala Center (Tibetan), 245
New Orleans Zen Temple (Soto Zen), 251
New York Shambhala Center (Tibetan), 247
Newport Mesa Zen Center, 257
Nibbana and mindfulness, 11, 65
Nichirin Daishonin, 266
   "Lotus Sutra, The," 190–91
Nichirin Mission of Hawaii, 256
Nichirin Order of North America, 258
Nichirin Temple of Chicago, 253
Nirvana, 31
Nisargadatta, Sri, 99
Nondoing, 100
Nonself (anatman), 31
Nonsense, 86
Nostrils, 116, 151
   nexus point of, 155, 155–56, 161, 236
Not-thinking, 34, 38

Objects of mind. See Mind-objects
Ocamora Foundation, 258
"Om mani padme hum" (mantra), 188–89
Omniscient states, 52
One Zendo [Soto Zen/Gay, Bisexual], 255
One-breath meditation, 57–59
"Oneness of Duality, The" (Suzuki), 138–41
One-pointedness, 161, 231. See also Nostrils, nexus point
"Open the Hand of Thought" (Uchiyama), 121–22
Opening what is closed, 73–74

Pain, 65
   dharma, 74
   healing of body, 94–96
   sensations of, 73–74
Palden Sakya Center, 247
Pali language, xiv
Panna (higher understanding), 44, 207
Paramitas (virtues), 189
Past, 155, 162
Patrul Rinpoche, 266
   "Mani," 188–89
Perceptions as skandha, 15
Permanance versus impermanance, 77–79
Personal power (joriki), 51

Personal transformation, 61
Phenomena (dharmas), 16, 42
Philadelphia Buddhist Association, 246
Philosophy, Buddhism as, 103
Physical happiness, 213
Place for meditation, 108
Plum Tree Zendo, 246
Portland Shambhala Center (Tibetan), 256
Postures for meditation, 111–12, 113, 126–43
Prajnaparamita philosophy, 33
Prayer, 19
Present moment, 177–79, 182. See also Here-and-now
Present-time process, breathing as, 155, 161–62
Problems in meditating, 216–40
Providence Zen Center, 245
Psychic energy center, 208–10
Pure Land meditation, 32

Quaker meetings, 124

Rahula (son of Buddha), 66–68
Reactions
  automatic, 29
  balancing of, 74–76
Reading, inspirational, 22, 108
Reality, 71, 86
  and enlightenment, 6
  exploration of, 76–79
  and illusion, 154
  nature of, 90–93
Relaxing the mind, 10
Releasing the mind, 9–10
Religions and meditation, 7
Renunciation, 176
Restlessness, 220, 222–30
Retreats, 22, 123–25
Rigpe Dorje Center (Tibetan), 254
Rinzai Zen meditation, 34, 169
Rochester Zen Center, 248
Roshi (teacher), 34–35

Sacred phrases, 186. See also Mantras
Sadhana (rituals), 35
Safety, 212
Salzberg, Sharon, 266
  "Exercise/Lovingkindness," 214–15
  "Metta Practice," 211–13
Samadhi (stillness), 41, 192
Samatha, 28, 83. See also Shamatha (calm abiding);
  Vipashyana (insight or higher vision)
Samsara, 6, 8, 188, 223

San Francisco Saraha Buddhist Center [Kadampa], 258
San Francisco Zen Center, 258
Sangha (community), 123–25
  "Sangha and Retreat" (Kornfield), 123–25
Sang-ngak-cho-dzong (Tibetan/Nyingma)
  California, 258
  New York, 247
Sanity, 90, 92
Sanskrit language, xiv
Sariputta, Venerable, 13
Sati (to dwell in mindfulness), 13
  "Satipatthana Sutta," 11, 13, 30
Seed mantra (baja), 36, 186
Self (atman), 31
Self-knowledge, 45
Sensations, labeling of, 109, 117–19
Sense desire, 15, 222–30
Sense of humor, 24, 25
Sense impressions, 73, 117–19
Sense organs, 15–16
Separatism, 98–99
Seven Factors of Awakening, 16, 144, 148–50
  "Seven-Point Posture" (McDonald), 133–37
Shamatha (Calm Abiding), 30–31. See also Samatha
Shambhala Center/Dharmadhatu (Tibetan), 249
Shasta Abbey [Soto Zen], 258
Shine-Lhatong, 36
Shingon Buddhist International Institute (Koyasan
  Shingon), 257
Shunyata (emptiness), 31, 35
Siddhartha Gautama. See Gautama Buddha
Simpleness of meditating, 107
Skandhas (aggregates), 15
Sleep, 226, 227
Sloth and torpor, 222–30
Snelling, John, 266
  "Buddhist Traditions of Meditation," 29–36
Snyder, Gary, 267
  "Just One Breath," 57–59
Sogyal Rinpoche, 267
  "Bringing the Mind Home," 5–10
  "Mind's Own Radiance, The," 216–18
Soho Zendo, 247
Sonoma Mountain Zen Center, 258
Sorrow, 65, 96
Soto Zen meditation (Shikan-taza), 34, 169
Sounds, 114, 118, 196–97
Southern Dharma Retreat Center (mixed), 249
Space for meditation, 108
Spencer Buddhist Meditation Group, 249
Spirit Rock Meditation Center (Vipassana), 261

Spiritual centers, 124

Spiritual life, growth of, 18

Springwater Center for Meditative Inquiry and
Retreats (mixed), 248

Stabilizing meditation, 200

Stone Creek Zendo (Soto Zen), 259

Stone Mountain Zendo, 249

"Stopping and Being Present" (Kabat-Zinn), 47–48

Stopping exercise, 49

Stranger, The (Camus), 70

Study centers for Buddhist meditation, 243–259

Suffering
duhkha, 31
in Four Noble Truths, 16
root of, 27, 93, 97
and samsara, 6

Sukhavati, Pure Land of, 32

Sung dynasty (China), 34

Support in community, 123–25

Sutra (discourse), 13

"Sutra on the Full Awareness of Breathing"
(Buddha), 144–50

Suzuki, Shunryu, 267
"For Enlightenment," 103–4
"Oneness of Duality, The," 138–41
"Swinging Door, The," 158–59

"Swinging Door, The" (Suzuki), 158–59

"Taming a Wild Elephant" (Gunaratana), 153–57

Tampa Karma Thegsum Choling (Tibetan Karma
Kagyu), 250

T'ang dynasty (China), 33

Tantric meditation, 35–36, 199

Taos Vipassana Sangha, 255

Tara (diety), 199

Tara Mandala (Tibetan), 255

Tathagata ("thus gone one"), 193

Teeth, 112, 113

Tekchen Choling (Tibetan/Gelugpa), 252

Theravada Buddhism, 42, 44

"Thinking in Pictures" (McDonald), 198–202

Thoughts
dropping, 87
labeling, 55–56, 87, 117–19
letting go of, 121–22
in meditation, 216–18, 231
nature of, 97–99

Three Cranes Zen Center, 247

Thynn Thynn, 267
"Attention to Emotions," 205–7
"Concentration and Meditation," 44–46

Tibetan Buddhist Center of Philadelphia, 246

"Tibetan Meditation Instructions" (Dalai Lama),
112–15

Time for meditation, 108, 115

"To Achieve Necessary Awareness" (Hanh), 69–71

"To Heal the Body, Heart, and Mind"
(Kornfield), 94–99

"To Investigate Reality" (Wallace), 90–93

"To Open, To Balance, To Explore" (Goldstein),
72–79

"To Pursue Your Vision" (Kabat-Zinn), 100–102

"To Transcend Everyday Consciousness" (Khema),
82–87

Tongue, 112, 113, 136

Traditional societies, 100

"Training of the Heart" (Goldstein), 208–10

Tranquillity, 91–93

Tranquillity practice, 173

Transcendental consciousness, 82–87

Transformation
of consciousness, 209
personal, 61

Transmigration, 193

Tricycle magazine, 243

Truth and meditation, 5

Ts'ao-tung (Japanese Soto), 33

Tse Chen Ling Center for Tibetan Buddhist
Studies, 258

"Tuning the Breathing" (Man-an), 151–52

Uchiyama, Kosho, 267
"Open the Hand of Thought," 121–22

Udumbara Zen Center Central (Soto Zen), 253

Unitarian Church North Zen Group, 252

Universal existence, 159, 194–95

Unsatisfactoriness (dukkha), 84

Vajra (full-lotus posture), 133–34

Vajradakini Buddhist Center (Kadampa), 254

Vajrapani Institute (Tibetan), 258

Vajrayana practice, 199

Value of meditation, 100–102

Village Zendo, 246

Vipashyana (insight or higher vision), 30–31. See
also Samatha

"Vipassana Meditation Instructions" (Goldstein),
116–20

Vipassana (penetrative seeing/insight), 27–28, 45,
83

Virtues (paramitas), 189

Vision and meditation, 100–102
Visions, 50
Visualization, 19, 198–204
    creative, 36

Waking dream, 29
Walking exercise, 173–76
Walking meditation, 166–76
Wallace, B. Alan, 268
    "To Investigate Reality," 90–93
Wat Buddharangsi [Vipassana], 250
Water, 66–67
"Ways of Using the Breath" (Khema), 160–62
Westchester Buddhist Meditation Group, 247
"What Practice Is" (Beck), 53–56
"What Practice Is Not" (Beck), 50–52
"What to Do with Your Body" (Gunaratana), 126–32
"When the Mind Wanders" (Gunaratana), 233–38
White light meditation, 203–4
Wichita Buddhist Meditation Groups, 254

Yasutani Roshi, Hakuin, 33, 268
    "Counting Breaths," 231–32
    "Kinhin," 168–69
Yellow Springs Dharma Center, 251
Yidam (diety), 35, 36

Yoga, 22
    hatha, 136–37
Yogacara philosophy, 33
Yogic methods, 35

Zazen and samadhi, 42, 43
Zazen (sitting meditation), 33, 34
Zen Affiliate of VT, 245
Zen Buddhist Temple (Korean Zen) of Ann Arbor, 252
Zen Buddhist Temple (Korean Zen) of Chicago, 253
Zen Buddhist Temple (Korean Zen) of Toronto, 259
Zen Center of Hawaii, 256
Zen Center of Hot Springs, 254
Zen Center of Los Angeles, 51, 257
Zen Center of Syracuse, 248
Zen Center of New York, 246
Zen Community of Oregon, 256
Zen Fellowship, 259
Zen Group of Reading Aikido Makoto Dojo, 246
Zen meditation, 33–35, 37–39
Zen Meditation Center of Hollywood, FL, 250
"Zen Meditation Instructions" (Dogen), 111–12
Zen Mountain Center, 257
Zen Mountain Monastery, 248